MISSISSIPPI RIVER

Text by
Rebecca Pittman

Photos by
Andrea Pistolesi

BONECHI

CONTENTS

MISSISSIPPI RIVER
Project and editorial conception: Casa Editrice Bonechi
Picture research: Monica Bonechi
Graphic design and Make-up: Serena de Leonardis

Text: Rebecca Pittman
Map: Studio Grafico Daniela Mariani, Pistoia
Editing: Anna Baldini

© Copyright 1996 by Casa Editrice Bonechi - Florence - Italy
ISBN 88-8029-420-2

Sole Agent in North America: Ilaria Sartori
255 Centre Street - 6th Floor - New York, NY 10013 - Tel.: (212)343-1464
Fax: (212)343-8045

Printed in Italy by Centro Stampa Editoriale Bonechi.

Photos from the archives of Casa Editrice Bonechi taken by
Andrea Pistolesi

The historical photos on pages 3 (below), 5 and 103 are courtesy of
Mississippi Department of Archives & History.
*Photos on pages 4 (below), 92 and 93 (center, right):
images of Elvis used by permission, the* Estate of Elvis Presley.
Photos on pages 31 (below), 32 and 33 by Jerry Stransky: © Cartwheell Co.
Photo on pages 48-49: © Joe Luman.
The Great River Road© *logo is a courtesy of MRPC.*

*   *   *

*I*n the memorable opening sentences of Life on the Mississippi, *Mark Twain writes that the Mississippi River is "not a commonplace river, but on the contrary is in all ways remarkable."* First published in 1863, these lines are in all ways accurate – then and today.

Meandering through the heart of America, the Mississippi River flows 2,348 miles from its Minnesota source to the Gulf of Mexico. Along the way, the river borders 10 states, while draining water and sediment from 31 states and two Canadian provinces. Taken as a whole, the Mississippi River system approaches 12,350 miles in length. Encompassing the Missouri and Ohio rivers (among many others), this is by far the world's longest river system. The Mississippi River Valley is approximately 35,000 square miles in size and 600 miles long. The Mississippi River's basin covers 41 percent of the continental U.S., more than 1,245,000 square miles. It is the 3rd-largest drainage basin in the world, after the

The Mississippi River at its source at Lake Itasca.

watersheds of the Amazon and Congo rivers. Every day, the Mississippi River lifts two million tons of sediment from its basin lands and transports this load to the ocean.

The Mississippi River **Headwaters** run 500 miles from the river's Minnesota source to Minneapolis/St. Paul. Here, at the Falls of St. Anthony, begins the **Upper River**, which stretches through the nation's heartland to where the Ohio River merges with the Mississippi at Cairo, Illinois. The massive, broad **Lower River** flows from here 1,000 miles to its narrow **Delta** below New Orleans. Alongside much of the Upper and Lower River, the **Great River Road**© provides motorists, hikers, and bicyclists with an impressive scenic and historic thoroughfare.

The Mississippi is a romantic river with a romantic history. In a futile and tragic search for gold, Spanish explorer Hernando De Soto and his conquistadors be-

A grand expedition of European explorers confronts a band of Indians at the river's edge.

came the first whites to encounter the river, on May 21, 1541—probably from a bluff south of Memphis. De Soto, however, soon died from a fever. A handful of his men, tattered survivors of a once-grand expedition, escaped downriver on makeshift rafts to the Gulf of Mexico and, ultimately, to a Spanish fort. For more than 100 years afterwards, the existence of the river was clouded by myth and misinformation. Indians described a "great water" to European traders, who fervently hoped that this was the fabled Great Western Sea, a direct trading link to the riches of China. But in 1673 two Frenchmen, Father Jacques Marquette and Louis Joliet, explored the Mississippi from what is now the Wisconsin River down to the Arkansas River, establishing its north-south course. René Robert Cavelier, Sieur de La Salle, led a team that entered the Mississippi at the Illinois River and floated all the way down to the Gulf in 1682. He claimed the whole river and its tributaries for Louis XIV. A hundred years later, Spain briefly gained dominion over this vast territory. But the Louisiana Purchase in 1803 once and for all decided the Mississippi's American identity.

The various races and nationalities who at one time or another lay claim to the Mississippi River gave this body of water many names. The early Spanish explorers christened it "Rio del Espiritu Santo" (River of the Holy Spirit). Later conquistadors repeatedly renamed the river, dubbing it the "Rio Grande," "Rio Escondido" (Hidden River), and "Pilazido" (Palisades). The French gave it several names: "Colbert," after a contemporary politician; "St. Louis," after the patron saint of the king; and "Immaculate Conception." "Mississippi" is an Indian word, translated as "Big River" or "Father of Waters." Mark Twain (real name, Samuel Langhorne Clemens) in Life on the Mississippi records the use of a less flattering nickname: the "Great Sewer." Today the river is known colloquially as "Ole Man River," the "Muddy Mississippi," or the "Mighty Mississippi."

Clues to the presence of an advanced Indian civilization existing around 500-1300 A.D. can be found along the river. Archaeologists show that the Mississippi Valley was home to tribes who used relatively sophisticated agricultural techniques that allowed them a sedentary, rather than nomadic, way of life. With a highly-ordered social structure, these sun-worshipers traded with tribes as far away as the Gulf of Mexico. They were accomplished potters and artists – and they were consummate mound builders. This most striking evidence of their culture can be seen today all along the Mississippi. The **Cahokia Mounds State Historic Site**, along the river in Illinois near St. Louis, encompasses 85 mounds, including 100-foot-tall **Monks Mound**, the country's largest. Nearly 200 burial mounds – some shaped like bears and birds – can be found at **Effigy Mounds National Monument** in Marquette, Iowa. Just outside Natchez, Mississippi, the 35 foot-high **Emerald Mound** is the 2nd-largest ceremonial mound in the U.S.

Top: Hannibal, Mark Twain House and Museum.

Bottom: Elvis Presley, the King of Rock and Roll.

The Mississippi River has long been the source of colorful legends and su-perstitions. Chippewa Indians say the skeletal wraith of a young brave haunts the river's shore near Crow Wing in Minnesota, scene of a famous bat-tle between the Chippewa and the Sioux. A symbol of death, the huge, fearsome Piasa Bird is part of the mythology of several tribes along the Mississippi. The warrior Hiawatha, immortalized in Henry Wadsworth Longfellow's The Song of Hiawatha, figures in both Indian and pioneer lore. There's good reason to believe that the name of the river's source, Lake Itasca, is not strictly from Latin – as most his-tory books contend – but comes in part from the Indian story of Hiawatha's daughter, I-teska. According to legend, she was kid-napped by the god of the under-world, and her tears became the great river. The discoverer of the Mississippi's source (and the man who created the word "Itasca" from two Latin words), Henry R. Schoolcraft, relates her story in his poem: On Reaching the Source of the Mississippi River in 1832:

Ha! truant of western waters! Thou
who has
So long concealed thy very
sources, flitting shy.
Now here, now there – through
spreading mazes vast
Thou art, at length, discovered to
the eye....
As if, in Indian myths, a truth there
could be read,
And these were tears, indeed, by
fair Itasca shed.

It has been reasonably speculated that Schoolcraft adapted this Indian myth to Latin terms in order to fashion a name for his momen-tous discovery.
Tall tales of more outrageous char-acters also loom large in river folk-lore. Outlaws and pirates like Jean Lafitte occupy a special chapter in the river's mythology, much of it based upon fact. The well-docu-

Historical glimpses of a 19th-century Mississippi River steamboat, loading dock, and a flood.

5

mented crimes of the sadistic Harpe brothers are especially grisly. Likewise, the Murrell Clan of eastern Tennessee was feared from New Madrid, Missouri, to Vicksburg. More lovable – and far-fetched – Whiskey Jack was said to be a Paul Bunyan of the river, huge and strong as an ox. Bob Hooter was a legendary Mississippi Delta coon hunter. Probably the most famous river rascal was the hard-drinking yarn-spinner Mike Fink, the "King of the Mississippi Keelboatmen." Among Fink's notorious exploits: swallowing a buffalo robe to provide a new "coat" for his whiskey-eroded stomach.

Music is an essential aspect of the river's culture. The profoundly expressive idiom of slaves, early music along the Mississippi evolved into several important American genres. From ragtime in St. Louis, to the blues in Memphis and the Mississippi Delta, to jazz in New Orleans – music has always flowed along the great river. The beginnings of popular music today can be traced back to powerful songs hollered in Delta cotton fields or sung on bustling river docks.

But the Mississippi's most enduring symbol is the steamboat. Its invention in the early part of the 19th century sparked a boom in river commerce that lasted until the Civil War. In 1814, 21 steamboats docked in New Orleans; in 1833, the city recorded the arrival of more than 1,200 paddlewheelers. For all its popularity, however, the 19th-century steamboat was a very dangerous mode of transportation. (At one time the life expectancy of a paddlewheeler was only five years. The first steamboat on the Mississippi, the New Orleans, hit a snag in the river and sank after only three years in commission.) Horrific boiler explosions and accidents were commonplace. In Life on the Mississippi, Twain describes a catastrophic explosion on the steamboat

Above: Stepping stones bridge the shallow beginnings of the Mississippi River.

Two views of Minnesota's beautiful headwaters region.

More bridges cross the Mississippi at Minneapolis than at any other city along the great river.

Pennsylvania *sixty miles below Memphis that killed his brother and many*

others: "... four of the eight boilers exploded with a thunderous crash, and the whole forward third of the boat was hoisted towards the sky! The main part of the mass, with chimneys, dropped upon the boat again, a mountain of riddled and chaotic rubbish — and then, after a little, fire broke out. Many people were flung to considerable distances, and fell in the river...." The worst accident in the Mississippi's history occurred when the Sultana, a steamboat crammed with Union soldiers just released from a Confederate prison, exploded near Memphis and sank with over 1,000 lives lost. After explosions and fires, steamboat pilots feared colliding with half-submerged logs or old shipwrecks. Thanks to ever-shifting river beds and erratic water levels, riverboats were in constant danger of running aground.

But more and more, riverboats became a place to have fun, in spite of any dangers. By the mid-19th century, passenger paddlewheelers were often splendid boats lavishly outfitted with fine furniture, crystal chandeliers, oriental rugs, and music provided by elaborate calliopes — or whole orchestras. According to Twain, *"The*

Above: A barge locks through Alma's Lock and Dam.

A replica 19th-century steamboat at Alton's quaint riverfront.

The broad, massive lower river begins at the confluence of the Mississippi and Ohio rivers at Cairo, Illinois.

The Gateway Arch of St. Louis symbolizes the city as gateway to the American West.

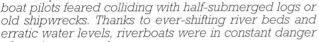

The Eads Bridge at St. Louis is the first significant bridge to span the Mississippi River.

Riverboat pleasure cruises are a popular Memphis pastime.

steamboats were finer than anything on shore. Compared with superior dwelling-houses and first-class hotels in the valley, they were indubitably magnificent, they were 'palaces.' " The grand tradition of luxury steamboating continues with a modern fleet of paddlewheelers cruising the Mississippi from Minneapolis/St. Paul to New Orleans. A National Historic Landmark, the Delta Queen has been on the river since 1926. The Mississippi Queen and the gargantuan, newly-christened Ameri-can Queen feature amenities that would have astonished Mark Twain: movie theaters, beauty shops, swimming pools. These days, however, most Mississippi River paddlewheelers serve as floating Las Vegas-style gambling casinos. The advent of dockside gambling has pumped cash and jobs into a number of towns along the Mississippi that otherwise possessed scant economic resources or prospects.

Twain calls the Mississippi the "crookedest river in the world," and it continues to twist and turn upon itself, creating endless sharp bends and secondary channels. Just as in his day, the protean river will often abandon the channels it cuts, creating shallow ox-bow lakes that over time can completely dry up and fill with sediment and vegetation. More than one town has found itself suddenly inland, thanks to the Mississippi's powerful capriciousness. But today the river's sinuous course is challenged by the U.S. Army Corps of Engineers, which works to correct its most egregious diversions. Around 1904, the Corps came to the rescue of Vicksburg after the fickle river moved away. The Corps cut a new channel, scoured by the nearby Yazoo River, and the city was back in business as a river port.

The Corps of Engineers turned its attention to the river early in the 19th century. In 1879, the U.S. Congress created the Mississippi River Commission, charged with flood control and improving river navigation and commerce. In 1922, $42 million was appropriated by Congress to build a system of locks and dams that would create a permanent shipping channel extending almost the entire length of the river. By 1944, the Corp had constructed 29 locks and dams

Rows of Mississippi cotton await the fall harvest.

The sounds of jazz provide a constant soundtrack to New Orleans' storied French Quarter.

Sunset at New Orleans; below, Natchez.

on the Upper River between Minneapolis/St. Paul and St. Louis. Mark Twain would surely be impressed with this man-made river ladder descending 420 feet over almost 700 miles.

Before the Corps went into action, riverboating along the Upper River was extremely difficult; vessels were in constant danger of running aground in shallow waters or being swept away by raging currents. Now the locks and dams keep the river deep enough for year-round shipping. The only potential disruption on the Upper River comes in winter, when ice can close the river as far south as Missouri.

Commerce on the river today is very big business. In 1940, Mississippi River traffic totaled 30 million tons of commodities. In 1993, that figure had ballooned to more than 600 million tons. Most commercial traffic on the river is transported by tremendous barges, some capable of holding over a million gallons of oil. High-powered modern towboats can push 40 or more barges, for a total capacity of 50,000 to 60,000 tons of cargo – typically steel, grain, ore, petroleum products, or chemicals.

Every spring the river floods. Just how much, how long, and where have been vexing questions for centuries. The explorer De Soto witnessed a severe Mississippi flood occurring in 1543, the first ever recorded. The epic flood of 1927 was the most disastrous in the river's history, inundating almost 26,000 square miles and killing more than 200 people. But even in mild years, erratic flooding has bedeviled rivermen, river towns, and farmers. The Corps of Engineers battles flooding in the Mississippi Valley today with a 2,203 mile-long system of levees, floodwalls, and other water control structures.

The Mississippi's "birdfoot" delta is a huge brackish swamp rich with plant and animal life.

The first commissioned steamboat docked at New Orleans in January 1812.

GREAT RIVER HEADWATERS

At placid Lake Itasca, 100 miles from the Canadian border and 1,475 feet above sea level, the Mississippi River begins its existence as an inauspicious trickle, nine paces wide and ankle-deep. Barefoot tourists by the thousands come to this spot all summer long to make the historic crossing, Paul Bunyan-like, tramping over the smooth, rounded stepping-stones placed by park rangers to create a bridge. Typically contrary, the river flows north from Lake Itasca, then east through the Mississippi Headwaters country, a wilderness of more than 1,000 lakes, rivers, and streams. At the resort town of Bemidji, the river makes a sharp right turn and heads east. For 120 miles the Mississippi puddle-jumps from lake to lake until reaching the city of Grand Rapids, where it finally begins its serpentine 2,500-mile journey south.

The location of the Mississippi's source was a mystery that confounded western explorers for centuries. It is widely believed that, while sailing along coastal waters of the Gulf of Mexico in 1519, Spanish explorer Alverez de Piñeda became the first European to see the mouth of the river. But it would be more than 300 years before the river's Minnesota headwaters were discovered by a white man. Over the centuries, in what became a celebrated geographical mystery, a stream of frontier explorers made arduous journeys through the rugged northern terrain in search of the Mississippi's origins. In August 1805, Lt. Zebulon M. Pike and 20 volunteers set out from St. Louis with orders to explore the river headwaters and secure American authority over the region. Pike was to become a famed explorer of the American West (he is the namesake of Pike's Peak in

Who can resist wading the nine steps across the humble origins of the Mississippi at Lake Itasca?

The scenic Mississippi headwaters offer a superb and challenging stream for canoeing.

Following pages: left, this stream of water leaving Lake Itasca will reach the Gulf of Mexico in 60 days; right, placid Lake Itasca in the morning mist.

the Rocky Mountains) and a war hero, dying as a general in the War of 1812. In search of the river's source, he and his small party suffered through a harsh winter camped near Minneapolis' Falls of St. Anthony, and later mistakenly declared Leech Lake – about 80 miles from Lake Itasca – the Mississippi's source. But this expedition was hardly ill-fated. Pike planted the American flag throughout the region, while forcing the British flag, when encountered, to be taken down. This action proved crucial in later negotiations where Great Britain lost its claim to the northern and western U.S. frontier. Michigan territorial governor Lewis B. Cass organized the next search for the Mississippi's source in 1820. He got as far as the body of water now know as Cass Lake, 100 miles below Lake Itasca. Italian exile Giacomo Constantino Beltrami came closest to discovering the

river headwaters in 1823. A decidedly off-beat adventurer, he broke away from a U.S. Army surveying expedition to search for the Mississippi's source. Accompanied by a few Indian guides and equipped with little more than a canoe and a burning desire to become a world-famous explorer, Beltrami was soon deserted by his Indian companions. Still he proceeded up Red Lake River. At a Chippewa village on Red Lake, he met a half-breed who promised to show him to the river's source. But Beltrami was led to the wrong lake, which he named Lake Julia, after Countess Giulia Medici Spoda. Safely returned to civilization, he was unable to prove to anyone's satisfaction that he had discovered the source of the Mississippi. (He perhaps overdid things by claiming to have found the Red River's source, as well.) Finally, the mystery was solved in 1832 by the miner-

Once decimated by logging, the forest surrounding Lake Itasca has now largely recovered.

The headwaters region is dotted by ponds, spruce bogs, and lakes dug long ago by retreating glaciers.

Following pages:
Itasca Park's towering stands of red and white pines are home to many varieties of wildlife, including bald eagles.

alogist and Indian agent Henry Rowe Schoolcraft, who had been a member of Lewis B. Cass' party. In a well-planned, well-equipped journey that took just a week, Schoolcraft was guided by Chippewa Chief Ozawindeb to the antler-shaped lake that is the river's source. In celebration, Schoolcraft raised the American flag, fired off a round of gunfire, and patched together syllables from two Latin words, "veritas caput" ("true head"), to create the new name of his discovery: Lake Itasca. In his own account of this momentous discovery, Schoolcraft wrote: "We followed our guide down the sides of the last elevation with the expectation of momentarily reaching the goal of our journey. What had been long sought, at last appeared suddenly. On turning out of a thicket, into a small weedy opening, the cheering sight of a transparent body of water burst upon our view. It was Lake Itasca – the source of the Mississippi." Fifty years later, however, his find was called into question by another explorer, who

claimed that the true source of the Mississippi River was a lake above Lake Itasca. In 1888, the Minnesota Historical Society resolved the issue by sending the lawyer and historian Jacob V. Brower to survey and map the remote region. Brower affirmed Schoolcraft's achievement, and in so doing acquired a life-long passion, protecting the area from ruin at the hands of the logging industry. Thanks to his dauntless efforts, the Minnesota State Legislature established **Itasca State Park** in 1891. He was the park's first commissioner, serving four years without pay.

For the rest of his life, Brower worked to stop logging in the park. But only after the last tree was cut did Lake Itasca become a genuine public preserve, off-limits to commercial interests. Happily, many thousands of acres of northern Minnesota's wilderness are protected today, and the forest around Lake Itasca has largely recovered from the ruinous excesses of Brower's era.

Itasca Park's many wilderness trails guide visitors through this enchanting wilderness.

ITASCA STATE PARK

Itasca State Park covers 32,000 acres, about 50 square miles of preserved woodlands around Lake Itasca. Towering stands of red and white pines, rounded low hills, ponds, spruce bogs, and lakes dug long ago by retreating glaciers define the landscape. The first white men acquainted with this wilderness hill country, French fur traders, called the area *hauteurs des terres* or "heights of land." The region is a watershed draining three ways: south to the Gulf of Mexico, north through the Red River to Hudson Bay, and east through Lake Superior to the Atlantic Ocean. Called Antler Lake by the Chippewa Indians, Lake Itasca is long, thin, and shaped like an upside-down "Y." The nascent Mississippi flows out of the northern prong; a drop of water leaving here will reach the Gulf in 60 days. But the river is barely navigable in its uppermost stream – even a canoe has difficulty traveling the shallow, frequently dammed 500 miles from the river's source to its official head of navigation at Minneapolis/St. Paul. Now the waters are a fisherman's dream, and wildlife flourishes along this peaceful stretch of the river:

blue herons, owls, bald eagles, fox, deer, raccoons, skunks, river otters, beavers, even bears.

Several hundred years ago, the land now called Minnesota was bitterly contested by two Indian tribes, the Chippewa (whose name had been corrupted by Europeans from the original "Ojibwe") and the Sioux, also called Santee Dakota. The Chippewa had migrated to the region from their eastern homeland, pressured by white settlers and by the powerful, war-like Iroquois who lived in what was to became New York state. For almost two centuries the Chippewa and the Sioux waged war for dominion over Mississippi headwaters hunting grounds. Finally, the Sioux were decisively defeated at the Battle of Crow Wing in 1768 by Chippewa better-armed with steel knives and French muskets. Today the Chippewa live on **Leech Lake Indian Reservation**, which includes Leech Lake, Cass Lake, and Lake Winnibigoshis. (Leech Lake is the largest lake in the area; the Mississippi flows through the other two.) Practicing ancient techniques, they still use canoes to harvest wild rice, an important part of

The Mississippi River flows through Lake Winnibigoshish, part of the Leech Lake Indian Reservation.

their economy. In the last few years, however, a wholly different and much more lucrative industry has sprung up on Chippewa tribal lands – casino gambling.

Itasca State Park is well-developed, with lodging, boat landings, a museum, picnic area, many hiking trails, bike rental, campgrounds, clubhouse, and a swimming beach. Historic **Douglas Lodge** was built between 1904-1906 and is located overlooking the east prong of Lake Itasca. Open Memorial Day weekend to mid-October, Douglas Lodge offers reasonably-priced rooms, suites, and cabins – plus meeting rooms, dining rooms, and gift shops. Completely restored in 1992, the **Mississippi Headwaters Hostel** is run by Hostelling International.

The massive log and stone **Forest Inn** was erected by the Veteran's Conservation Corps at the end of the Great Depression. Today it serves as a meeting room and information site featuring pamphlets and a large model of the park. On the eastern side of the lake's northern prong, **Brower Inn** offers a beautiful view of the water, plus food service. The park's swimming beach is just south of Brower Inn.

Early French traders call this country-side hauteurs des terres or "heights of land."

Wilderness Drive is an 11-mile, one-way road heading west from the headwaters past the 2,000-acre **Itasca Wilderness Sanctuary**, a Registered National Landmark by the National Park Service. A five-mile paved bike trail runs along the east side of the lake from Douglas Lodge to the Mississippi Headwaters; bike rentals are available. Of the park's 24 hiking trails, the busiest is the **Headwaters Trail**, which leads to the point where Lake Itasca becomes the stream that is the Mississippi River's source. Among the roads less traveled are **Dr. Robert's Trail**, which goes through a bog and past an old timer's cabin, and the **Mary Lake Trail**, which begins below Forest Inn and runs to a deer enclosure. Forgot to pack your hiking boots? The *Chester Charles* is also available for serene sight-seeing cruises on the lake.

The river flowd from Itasca State Park to Bemidji, which calls itself the "First City on the Mississippi." Here enjoy both winter and summer activities by Lake Bemidji, or the approximately 400 fishing and recreational lakes nearby. And, of course, get your picture taken standing next to the 18-foot statues of Paul Bunyan and his pet blue ox, Babe.

The Minneapolis waterfront has been transformed into the exciting Mississippi Mile.

MINNEAPOLIS

The Upper Mississippi River begins around Minneapolis/St. Paul, the river's official head of navigation. Here is where the river becomes a commercial – as well as geographical – force to be reckoned with.

Observers love to delineate the differences between Minneapolis and its fraternal twin city, St. Paul, which grew up directly across from one another on the Mississippi. While only seven years younger than its rival, Minneapolis is said to be the more modern of the two, known for its sleek skyscrapers, cosmopolitan malls, and for its reputation as a commercial and industrial center.

In that same progressive spirit, Minneapolis has transformed its riverfront into the **Mississippi Mile**, with acres of parks, walking paths, bikeways, cobblestone streets, gourmet restaurants, nightclubs, shops, hotels, and more. The historic **Pillsbury "A" Mill** here, once powered by the river, was in its day said to be the largest flour mill in the world. The **Nicollet Island Pavilion and Amphitheater** show-

cases special summer events. From **Boom Island Park**, the **Anson and Betsey Northrup Paddleboats** launch daily river excursions from Memorial Day to Labor Day, including an inviting Sunday brunch cruise. Along the Mississippi Mile's downtown side, the **St. Anthony Falls Heritage Zone** is mapped for walking tours of its historic district and archaeological ruins. Or take it easy and ride the **Rivercity Trolley**, which conducts narrated tours of the Mississippi Mile and downtown Minneapolis in gasoline-powered replicas of old-fashioned trolley cars.

Six bridges span the river along the Mississippi Mile, including the renovated **James J. Hill Stone Arch Bridge**, built in 1883, and now open to walkers, bikers, and the trolley. The new **Father Louis Hennepin Bridge** has gone up where a first bridge across the Mississippi was constructed in 1855. More river history can be found at what's left of the **Falls of St. Anthony**, once a turbulent 16-foot cascade blocking

Powered by the river, the Pillsbury "A" Mill was once the world's largest flour mill.

On the following pages, A night view of Minneapolis' riverfront.

upstream traffic. In 1680 Father Hennepin became the first European to discover the falls, which he named after his patron saint, Anthony of Padua. Minneapolis grew up around these falls, which were harnessed to waterwheels powering flour and timber mills. From the "golden era" of the 1880s to the 1930s, Minneapolis was the flour milling capital of the world; today the **Minneapolis Grain Exchange** is one of the world's largest cash grain markets. The docile falls are now tamed by the **U.S. Army Corp of Engineer's Upper St. Anthony Lock and Dam**, the first of 29 locks and dams along the upper Mississippi. Here see the river hard at work: the observation deck offers a ring-side seat, as barges and other craft lock through.

St. Anthony's Falls were once, in fact, located near **Fort Snelling**, but the soft limestone beneath the river here erodes easily. Remarkably, this erosion has pushed the falls more than four miles north of the point where they were first known to be. Were it not

Established in 1819, Fort Snelling is considered the historic heart of Minnesota.

for Corps reinforcements, St. Anthony's Falls might have washed away entirely. Stalwart Fort Snelling, however, still stands where it was established in 1819, atop a bluff at the point where the Minnesota River meets the Mississippi. But the old stone fortress, the historic heart of Minnesota, no longer stands guard over a dangerous, unknown frontier. An active Army post until 1946, Fort Snelling is today a state park and National Historic Landmark. From May through October the fort is open to the public, complete with costumed "soldiers" recreating outpost life.

Within the city there are 22 lakes and 153 parks linked by 45 miles of paved paths, along which walking, jogging, biking, and sailing are choice summer activities. Winter pastimes include ice skating, cross-country skiing – even baseball on ice! Professional sports are a year-round passion; the city's **Hubert H. Humphrey Metrodome** is home base for both the **Minnesota Vikings NFL** football team and the **Minnesota Twins** baseball club.

Shopping in Minneapolis has been elevated to something like Olympic sport, even in the coldest weather. Over 50 blocks of downtown are connected by a climate-controlled skyway system that protects consumers from the elements while linking world-class stores like **Saks Fifth Avenue** and **Neiman Marcus**. In particular, downtown's newly-renovated **Nicollet Mall** is a 12-block shopping and entertainment extravaganza. And speaking of extravagant: **Mall of America** is located immediately south of Minneapolis in the metro community of Bloomington. With 4.2 million square feet of shopping space, Mall of America is the country's largest enclosed retail and entertainment center.

For the artistically-inclined, Minneapolis is a cultural wonderland. The **Minneapolis Institute of Arts** is a widely-acclaimed comprehensive fine arts museum.

The **Walker Art Center/Minneapolis Sculpture Garden** houses an outstanding collection of modern art. The **Minnesota Symphony Orchestra** is supported by both twin cities, an example of the cooperation that has replaced an old rivalry.

The Twin Cities boast more live theaters than anywhere except New York City, with Minneapolis' Tony award-winning **Guthrie Theater** offering superb productions of classical works. The **Historic Orpheum Theatre** and the **Historic State Theatre** have been lavishly renovated and are host to everything from Broadway shows to rock concerts. Indigenous jazz, pop, and rock have fused into the "Minneapolis Sound." Now the soul of a $1.5 billion-a-year recording industry, the Minneapolis Sound is exemplified by the music of Prince and hot contemporary producers Jimmy Jam and Terry Lewis.

Frontier outpost life is recreated at Fort Snelling, now a state park and National Historic Landmark.

Its modern skyline notwithstanding, St. Paul is reminiscent of a classic European city.

ST. PAUL

When characterizing St. Paul, people use terms like "traditional," "old world," and "charming." Government is a focal point of life here, as is the family, and this is a city that takes great pride in its heritage. A venturesome magazine ad produced by St. Paul invites tourists to "visit one of the world's classic European cities." The same ad also describes St. Paul as a "Victorian city." And, indeed, (St. Paul's modern skyscrapers notwithstanding) numerous fancy towers, turrets, stone arches, and baroque domes endow the city with a vibrant sense of the past. This is especially true along St. Paul's **Summit Avenue**, the longest row of Victorian mansions in the country. The **James J. Hill House** on Summit, built by a 19th-century railroad baron, is the largest mansion in the Midwest. The 15-room late-Victorian **Alexander Ramsey House**, built by the first Minnesota territorial governor, is open to the public, with tour guides in period dress. Summit Avenue is also known as the "Avenue of Churches," with 16

churches along a 4.5-mile stretch. Located at the end of Summit is one of the largest churches in the country, the **Cathedral of St. Paul**, modeled after St. Peter's Basilica in Rome.

St. Paul was established in the late 1830s on the east bank of the Mississippi River near historic Fort Snelling. Originally a shantytown that grew up a mile or two downstream from the fort, the settlement was first called Pig's Eye, after Pierre "Pig's Eye" Parrant, a local French-Canadian fur trader-turned-saloon owner. In 1841, a chapel was built and dedicated to St. Paul, which in due time replaced Pig's Eye as the town's name. This was a most salutary change: St. Paul is a much more appropriate moniker for a territorial capital, which the town became in 1849. When Minnesota joined the Union in 1858, St. Paul became the state capital. The **Minnesota State Capitol Building** in St. Paul (completed in 1905) is a sight to see, featuring the largest unsupported marble dome in the world. This beautiful building was designed by

St. Paul became a territorial capital in 1849; in 1858, the city became Minnesota's state capital.

renowned local architect Cass Gilbert, who designed the U.S. Supreme Court building. Also patterned after St. Peter's in Rome, the Minnesota capitol dome is 223 feet high and constructed from 22 different kinds of marble. At the base of the dome is the *Quadriga*, a gilded statue of Prosperity driving a chariot drawn by four horses. In one hand she holds the state symbols; in the other, the Horn of Plenty. On the first floor, 142 feet beneath the great dome's ceiling, is the *Star of the North*, a large glass mosaic that allows light to shine through from the floors immediately above and below. Above the main entrance to the capitol building are six statues by sculptor Daniel Chester French, representing the six virtues: *Wisdom*, *Courage*, *Truth*, *Bounty*, *Integrity*, and *Prudence*. Free 45-minute tours of the state capitol are conducted daily. The four-story lobby of the 19-story art deco **St. Paul City Hall** houses the three-story *Vision of Peace* statue by Carl Milles. Carved from white Mexican onyx, the statue represents an

St. Paul boasts more than 4,000 acres of beautiful parks.

"The American Queen" is the newest and grandest riverboat on the Mississippi.

Indian god of Peace. **The Landmark Center**, located in downtown's beautiful **Rice Park**, was once a federal courthouse. Built in 1902, it now serves as a popular community arts center. St. Paul's gangster days are celebrated during special tours at the Landmark Center, once the scene of sensational gangster trials. A few blocks away, tree-lined **Lowertown**, a 22-block downtown neighborhood bordered on the south by the Mississippi River, has been designated a shopping and entertainment district. Beautifully restored historic buildings and warehouses, art galleries, coffee houses, comedy clubs, bookstores, and innovative restaurants make this a hip and very livable "urban village," centered around the newly-rebuilt **Mears Park**.

On the western side of downtown, **St. Paul's Cultural District** contains more than 25 arts and cultural attractions. Area history is showcased at the dynamic new **Minnesota History Center**, which opened in 1992. The huge building is itself is a widely-praised architectural jewel. Inside are historical displays (be sure and see "Minnesota A-Z"), the "Home Places" multi-media theater, a genealogical collection, archives, and more. The **Science Museum of Minnesota**, in downtown St. Paul, offers fun hands-on exhibits ranging from anthropology to zoology. The Science Museum is also home to the **William L. McKnight - 3M Omnitheater**, a thrilling visual experience. The new **Minnesota Children's Museum**, created for children ages six months to 12 years, is an imaginative educational treat. With over 20,000 square feet of space, the Children's Museum features four permanent galleries, including Habitot, where infants and toddlers can burrow through the homes of prairie animals; and World Works, where children can operate a crane or weave patterns on an 18-foot loom. The performing arts, from Broadway hits to lavish grand opera, have a dazzling, world-famous venue here at the **Ordway Music Theatre**, modeled after great European performing halls. The

The Minnesota State Capitol Building, modeled after St. Peter's Basilica in Rome, is the world's largest unsupported marble dome.

internationally acclaimed Ordway is also the home of the **St. Paul Chamber Orchestra**. St. Paul's **Great American History Theatre** produces original works on midwestern life and heritage. The **Fitzgerald Theater** is home to Garrison Keillor's popular *A Prairie Home Companion* show, broadcast on public radio.

St. Paul boasts more than 4,000 acres of safe, clean parks designed with mom, dad, and the kids in mind. Designed with the local winters in mind, **Town Square Park** in the Central Business District is completely enclosed – waterfalls and streams included. It is the world's largest indoor public park. (The city's five-mile downtown skyway is the longest public skyway system in the world.) **Mounds Park** is situated around six 2,000-year-old burial mounds for the ancient Hopewell Indians. An outstanding free zoo and Victorian floral conservatory are located in **Como**

Park, along with an 18-hole golf course, paddleboating, cross-country ski trails, and many other recreational delights. Summer concerts are held at the Lakeside Pavilion here. **Cass Gilbert Memorial Park** honors the acclaimed architect and favorite son, while offering one of St. Paul's grandest views of the Mississippi River.

The nation's oldest winter carnival, the **St. Paul Winter Carnival**, has been held downtown in Rice Park every January since 1886. Fantastic ice sculptures erected throughout the park are highlights of this festival, which transforms the long, bitter cold into a splendid winter tradition. In late summer more than a million visitors come to the 12-day **Minnesota State Fair**, held in St. Paul at the Minnesota State Fairgrounds. With 300 acres of entertainment, midway rides, and exhibits, this is one of the largest state fairs in the country.

The Upper and Lower Riverfront Park borders the Mississippi River at Prescott.

PRESCOTT

Prescott, Wisconsin's oldest river town, was founded in 1840 where the icy waters of the St. Croix River merge with the more dour Mississippi. This location made Prescott a strategic center of river traffic, in particular barges loaded with white pine harvested from great forests to the north. Here steamboats also deposited thousands of immigrants, who settled Wisconsin and Minnesota in the last century. Eventually, however, railroads had become the dominant mode of transportation, and Prescott's boom-times were over.

The town was named for Philander Prescott, a trapper from New York state who held claim to 1,200 acres in the area for soldiers from Fort Snelling, Minnesota. Prescott later operated the first ferry across the mouth of the St. Croix and married the daughter of a Sioux Indian chief, by whom he had nine children. An Indian interpreter for the U.S. government during treaty negotiations, he was engaged by the man who discovered the source of the Mississippi River, Henry R. Schoolcraft, to write about Sioux history and customs. Prescott was killed during an Indian uprising in 1862. His journal and writings remain an important record of northwestern frontier life. Prescott's new **U.S. Highway 10 Bridge** spans the St. Croix just as it meets the Mississippi. At **Mercord Mill Park**, at the confluence of these rivers, the **Prescott Bridge Gearhouse** displays the antiquated gear system that once raised and lowered an older bridge. The **Upper and Lower Riverfront Park** borders the river here, and includes a walkway and picnic area.

A public dock and boat launch are nearby. Visitors can find information on Prescott history and attractions at **Old City Hall** downtown, home to the new **Welcome & Heritage Center**.

Immediately above its mouth, the St. Croix River widens into beautiful Lake St. Croix. A 25-miles long recreational attraction, Lake St. Croix is protected by the National Wild and Scenic Rivers System.

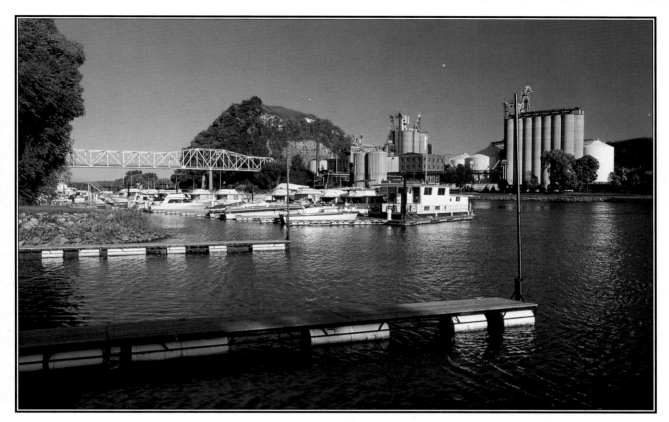

Red Wing is located on the north end of Lake Pepin, the largest lake formed by the Mississippi River.

RED WING

At Red Wing, below **Lock and Dam #3**, the river balloons to three miles across, creating Lake Pepin. Here there's less of a sense of the working river; commercial riverboats, barges, and the like are usurped by pleasure craft such as motorboats and sailboats (usually a rare sight on the Mississippi). The droves of Minnesotans who vacation here are river recreation experts: water skiing was invented on Lake Pepin in 1922, and ice fishing from heated huts becomes the main attraction in winter. Year-round, the area lays claim to what many call the best scenery along the river.

Red Wing sits at the north end of Lake Pepin. Many of the town's historic buildings are restored and featured on walking tours.

Learn about the Dakota Indians who lived here and the European immigrants who came afterwards, at the **Goodhue County Historical Museum**, located in Red Wing. Also, plan to visit the local pottery outlets for which the town is famous.

Swamps are part of the landscape all along the Mississippi River.

The U.S. Army Corps of Engineers Lock and Dam #4 at Alma locks through thousands of river vessels annually.

Following pages: Cornfields and grain silos define the agrarian landscape beyond Alma.

ALMA

Picturesque Alma likes to call itself the "New England of the Midwest," and it's got the scenery to prove it. Looking like a Vermont postcard, the little town (population 929) is nestled between the Mississippi River and majestic, wooded **Twelve Mile Bluff** – so-called because it could be seen from points far away on the river. In autumn the analogy becomes especially true; Alma has fall foliage to rival any part of New England. In late October thousands of graceful Tundra Swans en route south fly in and linger for several weeks. A wildlife observation platform at **Rieck's Lake Park** offers excellent bird-watching during "swan time" and all year long. Another unforgettable sight is the panoramic view from **Buena Vista Lookout and Picnic Area**, 500 feet above town. The scenery here is perhaps the loveliest along the Upper Mississippi River.

Most of Alma (comprised of two parallel streets) is on the National Register of Historic Places. Founded by Swiss immigrants in 1848, this charming village is the county seat, and was once an important stop for riverboats in Wisconsin's early logging days. Today, riverfront activity continues at the **U.S. Army Corp of Engineers Lock and Dam # 4**. Thousands of vessels lock through every year, and barges still regularly load and unload to service eight sawmills in the vicinity.

Recreational opportunities abound in Alma, with uncrowded river islands, two marinas, two full-service campgrounds, a 300-foot sandy beach, and outstanding fishing and deer hunting. During winter there's first-class snowmobile trails, cross-country skiing, or ice fishing. Festivals are big here, too, like the **Mark Twain River Festival**, with obligatory fence-painting and frog-jumping competitions, held every Labor Day weekend. The town's **Polka Festival** makes for a lively 4th of July, and each spring, Alma and 11 other communities stage the **Mississippi Valley Partners 85-Mile-Long Garage Sale**!

The Mark Twain House and Museum is filled with Twain memorabilia.

HANNIBAL

Hannibal is the epicenter of Mark Twain country, along Missouri's eastern Mississippi River border. Here Twain set the adventures of his venerable fictional characters Tom Sawyer, Huckleberry Finn, and Becky Thatcher – and here the writer himself actually lived from 1839 to 1857. Here, too, thousands of nostalgic tourists trek every year to experience a bygone America of barefoot boys, old-fashioned steamboats, and white picket fences.

The restored **Mark Twain Boyhood Home and Museum** commemorates Twain's Hannibal roots with memorabilia such as books, letters, and one of Twain's trademark white suits. Also on display in the two-story white frame house are Norman Rockwell paintings of scenes from *The Adventures of Tom*

Mark Twain's boyhood home stands next to a white picket fence said to have inspired Tom Sawyer's most famous exploit.

Sawyer and Huckleberry Finn. Next door is the whitewashed fence immortalized in Tom Sawyer. The home of Twain's childhood friend who was the inspiration for Becky Thatcher has also been restored and is open daily. See life-sized wax figures of Twain and his literary offspring at the **Haunted House on Hill Street**.

A statue of Hannibal's favorite son is the focal point of **Riverview Park**, situated on the bluffs above the Mississippi.

Getting around Hannibal is half the fun. Take the open-air Twainland Express, the horse-drawn Mark Twain Clopper, or the Hannibal Trolley. The Mark Twain transports sightseers on one-hour river cruises and dinner excursions.

A number of well-preserved pre-Civil War and Victorian homes can be found in Louisiana.

LOUISIANA

Some of the most thrilling scenery along the middle Mississippi River can be seen along down the Great River Road from Hannibal through Louisiana. For good reason, early French explorers along the Mississippi called this area the "Land of the Golden Hills." Now the great river broadens, expanding in some places to a mile wide. The steel-gray water is dotted with wild, densely-wooded islands, and lofty limestone bluffs rise from along the river's shoreline, some to as high as 600 feet. Here find some truly spectacular Lover's Leaps.

The pioneer founding fathers of the village of Louisiana first called their riverfront settlement Buffalo Fort. But the town was officially platted in 1818, and its name changed to Louisiana, a tribute to the Louisiana Purchase. The town's population now stands at 4,000 residents, many of whom are descendants of the original settlers.

By the 1860's tobacco played a large role in the town's economy, with 14 tobacco production facili-

Champ Clark Bridge spans the river at Louisiana.

ties located in the immediate area. Today, agriculture is still a strong local industry, along with the antique business and tourism. Sightseers especially come to see the town's **Downtown Central Business District**, a wonderfully preserved Victorian streetscape that has been placed on the National Register of Historic Places. Many of these streets are named for U.S. states (e.g. Tennessee St. and South Carolina St.) and are the sites of beautiful pre-Civil War and Victorian homes. The town also boasts seven well-maintained, shady parks. The **Louisiana Riverfront Park and Boat Ramp** is a popular public fishing spot and picnic area. The **Henderson-Riverview Park** at the crest of Main and Noyes streets in downtown Louisiana offers a magnificent lookout over the Mississippi River, along with benches, a playground, and a grand view of **Champ Clark Bridge**. On the southern end of the town's riverfront is the 3rd-oldest Mississippi river railroad bridge.

A visit to Elsah is like taking a step back in time to the 19th century.

The entire village of Elsah is on the National Register of Historic Places.

ELSAH

Until the Great River Road came through in 1965, the village of Elsah was decidedly off the beaten path. This isolation, however ultimately fortuitous, was not deliberate. In the mid-19th century, Elsah attemped to get in on the steamboat shipping boom, but her Mississippi River harbor wasn't sufficiently deep year-round. Then the village angled to become a bustling railroad town, but that effort was not a lasting success, either. Let us nonetheless give thanks for these failures, for rather than make progress, the entire town has remained largely untouched by the 20th century. Time seems to have forgot Elsah, which – lacking any significant modern structures – maintains a uniquely ubiquitous and charming 19th-century flavor.

Only 40 minutes from St. Louis, the entire village (population 125) is on the National Register of Historic Places. The little town was founded around 1852 by James Semple, who personally looked after the community – there was no official village govern-

ment until 1873, more than six years after his death. Semple controlled and maintained the waterfront, the street layout, the public facilities. Sometime after 1857 he built a school house. Today Elsah is a step back in time, a place for viewing the town's old stone structures, relaxing on a wide porch, antique shopping, and picnicking.

Mountain biking is a great way to tour the entire area; the **Sam Vadalabene Bike Trail** runs parallel to the Great River Road past Elsah, down to Alton. Bird lovers will want to keep an eye out for bald eagles, which winter here in the limestone bluffs along the Mississippi.

One mile below Elsah along the Great River Road, the illuminated statue of **Our Lady of The Waters** can be seen from the Missouri side across the Mississippi. The **Country Corner Fudge Store** in Grafton, Illinois, offers bike rentals. (Or get the folks at the gracious **Green Tree Inn** in Elsah to loan you a bicycle-built-for-two!).

Alton's downtown riverfront is an antique-lovers delight.

Alton's Melvin Price Lock and Dam #26 is a $1 billion U.S. Army Corps of Engineers project.

ALTON

The industrial city of Alton is located just above the celebrated confluence of the Mississippi and Missouri rivers. Flowing from the west, the Missouri (known as "Big Muddy") begins 4,032 feet above sea level in the Montana Rockies. It is the longest river in the nation – 2,714 miles. Even after converging, the two distinctly different rivers can be seen running side by side for 100 miles, the gray Mississippi along the east bank, the much muddier, brown Missouri along the west. A bit further upstream from this nexus, the Illinois River pours into the Mississippi.

While traveling along the Mississippi River through this area in 1673, French explorers Marquette and Joliet were dazzled by the sight of a monstrous bird painted by Indians on a limestone bluff near present-day Alton. A huge modern depiction of this mythical creature, the **Piasa Bird**, can be seen today from the Great River Road on a cliff facing the Mississippi River north of town. (The rocks bearing the actual bird

painting were quarried more than 100 years ago.) Originally an 18th-century French trading post, then a steamboat center, Alton is today an antique shoppers' mecca. In the years before the Civil War, the town was an important way station on the Underground Railroad. Prominent abolishonist Elijah P. Lovejoy edited a newspaper here and became an early martyr to the cause when murdered in 1837 by a mob, which threw his printing press into the river. A monument to Lovejoy is in the **Alton Cemetery**; the remains of his press have been salvaged and are on display at the Alton *Telegraph* newspaper offices. Historic downtown Alton was also the site of the last Lincoln-Douglas debate, in 1858, which attracted a crowd of 6,000 people.

Today, river traffic is helped through the Alton area by the newly-built **Melvin Price Lock and Dam #26**. This is the largest U.S. Army Corps of Engineers construction project, with a price tag of $1 billion-plus.

The Gateway Arch frames the St. Louis skyline.

Previous pages: The Mississippi and Missouri rivers, seen here at their confluence, merge to create the longest river in the U. S.

The river and the Gateway Arch, the largest man-made monument in the U. S.

ST. LOUIS

Dominating the St. Louis landscape, the **Gateway Arch** symbolizes the city's status as gateway to America's western frontier. The arch is located in the **Jefferson National Expansion Memorial**, a Mississippi riverfront park honoring President Thomas Jefferson's 1803 Louisiana Purchase, which sparked the massive western pioneer movement of the 19th century. For many settlers and fortune-hunters the odyssey west began in St. Louis, then the last American city before the vast Great Plains. Today the 630-foot, three-sided Gateway Arch is the tallest man-made monument in the U.S. Designed by Eero Saarinen and completed in 1965, this steel marvel is hollow, offering visitors who ride to its top a breathtaking view of the city and the river. Beneath the Arch, the **Museum of Westward Expansion** records a seminal chapter in American history. Also part of Jefferson National Expansion Memorial, **St. Louis' Old Courthouse** was the site of the famous

Dred Scott freedom suit, which helped ignite the Civil War. The Old Courthouse took a long time to build (from 1839 to 1862), thus its odd appearance, a combination of disparate architectural styles. Construction began when Greek Revival architecture was in vogue; by the time the dome was to go up, Italian Renaissance was stylish, and the two schools were incorporated. This is the first dome completed in the U.S. to be made of cast iron, its interior decorated with murals by painter Carl Wimar. Outside, a cast iron fence is whimsically decorated with turtles, in honor of a pet turtle kept for many years in a small nearby fountain. In front of the Old Courthouse, the impressive fountains of Kiener Plaza flank a statue of *The Runner*.

For St. Louis citizens the Gateway Arch also symbolizes the city's renewal and its revitalized connection with the Mississippi River. Founded in 1764 by Frenchman Pierre Liguest Laclède, St. Louis thrived

as a river port for more than 100 years. Its location a few miles south of the confluence of the Mississippi and Missouri rivers made the town a key trading post for fur and other goods shipped down the Missouri destined for New Orleans. The first steamboat docked here in 1817; records mark the arrival of something like 5,000 steamboats in 1860. As the 19th century drew to a close, however, the steamboat trade along the Mississippi River lost its primacy to the railroads. For many decades St. Louis suffered financially, its riverfront a shabby reflection of this decline. But St. Louis has experienced an economic and cultural resurgence. Modern industries like McDonnell Douglas Corporation and Anheuser Busch flourish here today, and its river trade is steady. Replicas of steamboat-era paddle wheelers now line the riverfront offering pleasure cruises and casino gambling – even floating fast food joints! Just north of the Gateway Arch along the river is **Laclède's Landing**, a nine-block historic district that has been restored to its cobblestone glory. Here are shops, unusual restaurants, and nightclubs featuring the ragtime music popularized by Scott Joplin, for which this city is renowned.

The story of graceful, triple-arched **Eads Bridge**, connecting St. Louis and East St.Louis, Illinois, is a classic chapter in the ongoing saga of man's effort to tame the "Mighty" Mississippi. Described by poet Walt Whitman as "a structure of perfection and beauty unsurpassable," Eads Bridge is the first significant bridge to span the Mississippi River. It is the world's first arched steel truss bridge – made with material supplied by Andrew Carnegie. At the time of its dedication it was the largest bridge ever built. Compressed air was key to the construction of Eads Bridge, the first such usage in the U.S. Its builder, Capt. James Buchanan Eads, was a 19th-century American hero, a self-educated engineering genius. He made a fortune salvaging sunken riverboats and riverboat cargo using a diving bell and other spe-

The Gateway Arch is the central feature of Jefferson National Expansion Memorial, a riverfront park.

American poet Walt Whitman described the Eads Bridge at St. Louis as "a structure of perfection and beauty unsurpassable."

cialized equipment he invented. During the Civil War Eads designed and manufactured the first fleet of Union ironclad gunboats. Because of his salvage work, he knew that simple bridge pilings could not withstand the powerful river current that flows past St. Louis at about 225,000 cubic feet of water per second, increasing to as much as one million feet per second during flood season. His solution was to sink the bridge's foundations to bedrock of then-unheard-of depths, 40 to 100 feet below the river bottom. His bridge was dedicated on July 4, 1874, and Eads' achievement remains today a remarkable feat of architecture and engineering.

One of America's most perceptive commentators had this to say more than 100 years ago regarding the outdoor public areas of St. Louis: "Forest Park....is beautiful and very extensive," noted Mark Twain in *Life on the Mississippi*, "and it has the excellent merit of having been made mainly by nature. There are other parks, and fine ones, notably **Tower**

A modern bridge across the river, with the Eads Bridge in the background.

Grove and the **Missouri Botanical Garden**; for St. Louis interested herself in such improvements at an earlier day than did most of our cities." Twain's observations were true when written, and since his day many generations of St. Louis residents and visitors have had cause to thank city fore-fathers for their timely regard for the great outdoors. Lush **Forest Park** is today the nation's 3rd-largest urban green space, after New York's Central Park and the Portland, Oregon, park system. Nonetheless, when first authorized in 1872, Forest Park was opposed by many citizens who considered its location too far from the city. Now a cultural and recreational marvel, the 1,300-acre park is the site of a number of impressive attractions, most notably the world-famous **St. Louis Zoological Park** (run for years by Marlin Perkins, Mr. Wild Kingdom). Home to more than 6,000 exotic animals, the St. Louis Zoo covers 83 acres and is free to the public, a remarkable bargain in this day and age. The first art museum west of the

On these pages and following, replica paddlewheelers on the Mississippi River.

Mississippi River, the **St. Louis Art Museum** (originally the Fine Arts Palace of the 1904 World's Fair) is also located in Forest Park, atop Art Hill. With a lovely neo-classical facade, the museum's middle section is patterned after the ancient Roman Baths of Caracalla. From the receipts collected during the 1904 Fair, the Jefferson gatehouse Memorial building was constructed. Today it houses the **History Museum**, which highlights the city's history from ancient times through the steamboat era on to the present. See especially mementos of Charles A. Lindbergh's epic 1927 solo flight across the Atlantic in the *Spirit of St. Louis*. In the heart of Forest Park, the **Jewel Box** greenhouse is an art deco mecca (built in 1936) for flower-enthusiasts, photographers, and anybody looking for an enchanting spot for an afternoon getaway.

Charming, anachronistic Tower Grove Park – located between Forest Park and the Mississippi River – was established in 1868 as an English Victorian walk-

ing garden, a gift to St. Louis from its greatest benefactor, Henry Shaw. Details of his auspicious arrival here are part of local lore: the 19-year-old Shaw, a native of Sheffield, England, first arrived in St. Louis on May 3, 1819, after a long trip from New Orleans aboard the steamboat *Maid of Orleans*. His Tower Grove Park was designed by Shaw and a fellow Englishman, James Gurney, imported from the Royal Botanical Gardens. Impressive, elaborate wrought-iron and stone gates frame the entrance, while the west gate brings to mind a medieval battlement.

Within the grounds are 12 fanciful gazebos and abundant fine statuary, including a copy of one of the *Weeping Lions* by Antonio Canova, which decorate the tomb of Pope Clement XIII in Rome. Tower Grove's three enormous bronze statues of Shakespeare, Columbus, and German naturalist Alexander von Humboldt are among the first large bronzes cast in the U.S. Henry Shaw himself planted

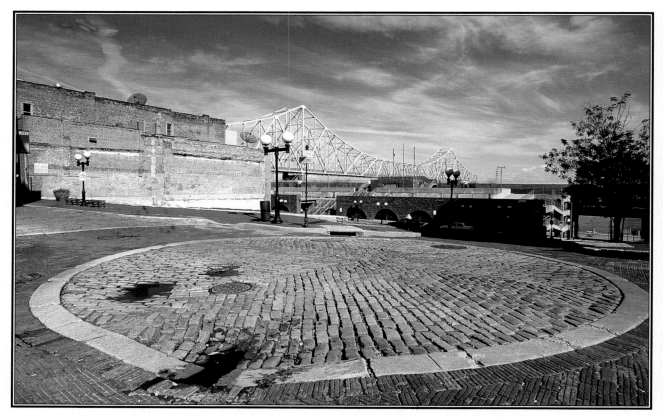

Laclèdes Landing in St. Louis is a nine-block historic riverfront entertainment district.

The St. Louis Old Courthouse was the site of the infamous Dred Scott trial, which helped ignite the Civil War.

the mulberry tree growing behind the statue of the Bard, a stripling transplanted from Stratford-on-Avon, England. In another area, a domed ornate bandstand, the scene of many Sunday afternoon concerts, is surrounded by marble busts on free-standing pedestals of Shaw's favorite composers. Even carefully designed (if not quite authentic) ruins of an English abbey can be found in this park, fashioned from charred stone blocks recovered from a burned hotel.

Adjacent to Tower Grove Park, the **Missouri Botanical Garden** is one of the world's great horticultural attractions. Also known as Shaw's Gardens, this beautiful and important garden is another part of Henry Shaw's extraordinary legacy to St. Louis. On these grounds Buckminster Fuller constructed his first geodesic dome, and Shaw's Italianate country house is here, restored and open to the public. Shaw's Gardens are also the site of the largest traditional Japanese garden in North America.

Turrets and all, 100-year-old **Union Station** looks as much like a medieval fortress as it does a railway station. Nowadays, however, Union Station in downtown St. Louis is no longer a train station, but a vibrant marketplace with more than 120 shops, restaurants, and entertainment facilities. Its Grand Hall, once the busiest passenger railroad terminal in the country, is now the beautifully renovated lobby of the Hyatt Regency Hotel. Just outside Union Station in Aloe Plaza is a dramatic group of lighted bronze fountain statuary called "The Meeting of the Waters." Symbolizing the confluence of the Mississippi and Missouri Rivers, the blithely nude Triton and naiads depicted by sculptor Carl Milles initially shocked many modest St. Louis citizens. Since its unveiling in 1941, however, *The Meeting of the Waters* has been one of the city's most beloved landmarks.

Ste. Genevieve's Bolduc House (built 1770) is a very fine example of an authentically restored Creole structure.

STE. GENEVIEVE

Ste. Genevieve residents obviously cherish their enduring customs and quiet Old-world way of life; in fact, the European flavor of the quaint village has hardly changed in 200 years. Local tourist brochures invite visitors to "walk the quiet streets....Experience the slower pace....Enjoy the peaceful calm of this 18th and 19th-century village." Three of the **Ste. Genevieve Catholic Church** bells still toll three times a day in call to prayer. Its fourth and smallest bell – the "death bell," named "Joseph" after the patron saint of happy death – is to this day rung upon the passing of parishioners. Travel literature, not surprisingly, also promotes Ste. Genevieve as a place to get a good night's sleep. At least six inviting historic bed and breakfasts provide such dreamy accommodations; one, the **Steiger Haus**, every year puts on over 100 popular murder mystery overnights – festive, *faux* murder dramas acted out and resolved by both staff and guests.

Father Jacques Marquette, who explored the Mississippi River with fellow Frenchman Louis Joliet,

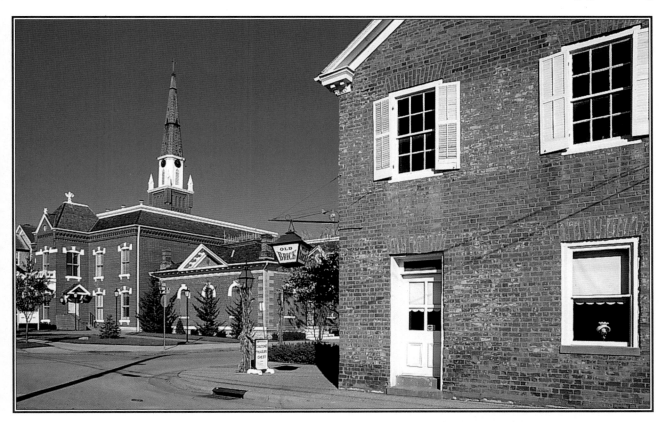

Church bells still call parishioners to prayer three times a day in Ste. Genevieve.

traveled to the present-day site of Ste. Genevieve in 1673. French miners and fur traders later established the town (located 60 miles below St. Louis) between 1725 and 1750, making it the oldest permanent settlement on the western side of the Mississippi. By the middle of the 18th century, Ste. Genevieve had become an important farming and trading center, a busy Mississippi River starting point for barges and keelboats shipping furs, lead, and other merchandise downriver to New Orleans. And after the French came an influx of immigrants from southern Germany who also made a significant and lasting mark on the local culture and architecture.

The **Ste. Genevieve Museum**, located downtown, features Indian relics dating to 12,000 B.C. The museum maintains an archive of significant old documents and Spanish land grants, plus artifacts from Missouri's first industry, the Saline Creek Salt Works. Also on display is a scale model of the Mississippi River railroad transfer boat, the *Ste. Genevieve*. The **Great River Road Interpretive Center** tourist infor-

A mural depicting frontier life decorates a building in St. Genevieve's historic downtown district.

mation office on Main St. directs tourists around town with displays and a movie, among other resources. The historic downtown district is also the site of a number of fine examples of 18th-and 19th-century French colonial architecture. The **Maison Guibourd-Valle House**, built around 1784, has been carefully restored and is open for tours conducted by costumed guides. Surrounded by grounds complete with a courtyard, old stone well, and rose garden, this handsome home is filled with elegant antiques. The attic, fitted with Norman truss and hand-hewn oak beams secured by wooden pegs, features changing exhibits and hanging dried herbs. The **Bolduc House**, a National Historic Landmark built in 1770 and moved to its present site in 1784, is widely hailed as the nation's earliest, most authentically restored Creole house. Open April-November, the Bolduc House shows original 18th-century furnishings, a stockade fence, frontier kitchen, and a medic-

The Felix Valle House State Historic Site was home to one of the town's earliest first families.

Following pages: The massive, broad Lower Mississippi River begins at its confluence with the Ohio River at Cairo, Illinois.

inal and culinary herb garden. The **Felix Valle House State Historic Site**, built in 1818, was the home to Felix and Odile Pratte Valle, members of one of Ste. Genevieve's early first families. Today this Federal-style limestone building is an authentically restocked Menard & Valle trading firm mercantile store. Visitors to the Felix Valle House can also see living quarters decorated with early Empire furnishings.

The upright cedar log walls of the **Amoureux House**, built ca. 1792 by Jean Baptiste St. Gemme Beauvais, are set directly into the ground in the rare *poteaux-en-terre* method of construction. The steeply-pitched roof is supported by heavy, hewn timbers forming a Norman truss. *Poteaux-en-terre* construction is also visible at the **Bequette-Ribault House**, which historians have dated to 1778. Combined French and American architectural influences are evident at the **Bolduc-Lemeilleur House**,

built in 1820. Fine early Federal furniture plus a vintage herb and fragrance garden are also interesting highlights of this tour home.

An unusual triangular fireplace at the **Green Tree Inn** – built in 1789 by Nicholas Janis, a friend of explorer George Rogers Clark – opens into three rooms. This structure, the first tavern west of the Mississippi, was the first Masonic meeting place in Missouri. The inn boasts original walnut shutters, doors, and mantels – and roof rafters made from 150 young walnut trees. Unfortunately, however, the Green Tree Inn is not open to the public. In fact, several important sites in Ste. Genevieve are strictly private residences – in most cases, home to direct descendants of the original French families who built them. The best time, then, to see these graceful structures is at the **Jour de Fête**, held annually in mid-August, when historic private homes are open for visitation.

Riverboats line the Memphis riverfront before the city's downtown skyline.

MEMPHIS

Memphis is a sprawling modern city, the country's second largest inland port. Cotton is still King here, and Memphis is a major national distribution center for goods of all kinds. (Drive around town and you'll pass by miles and miles of warehouses.) The city was founded in 1819 on the Mississippi River's high bluffs and was the home of the Chickasaw Indians until 1818, when their nation ceded West Tennessee to the U.S. It was the Chickasaw that gave the Mississippi its name: "Father of the Waters." Spanish explorer De Soto is believed to have first viewed the Mississippi from these bluffs in 1541; four centuries later, in 1986, a gala celebration was held in Memphis for the spectacular lighting of the Hernando De Soto Bridge.

Where the river steamboat trade once flourished, authentic replica paddlewheelers now offer pleasure cruises. *The Memphis Queen II*, *Memphis Queen III*, the *Island Queen*, *Belle Carol*, and the *Memphis Showboat* provide front-row seats for a riverside show, narrated by the captain of each boat. Among the points of interest: **Hernando De Soto Bridge**, **Harahan Bridge**, the **Frisco Railroad Bridge**, and the **Memphis-Arkansas Bridge**. Choose from one-and-a-half hour sightseeing cruises, a sunset dinner cruise, and a romantic moonlight dance cruise.

Today it seems as if the city took its cue from the expansive river, for Memphis is a city of broad avenues and spacious parks – 197 of them. Besides its role as a major trade and distribution, Memphis is one of the top ten wholesaling centers in the U.S. and is home to national corporations including Dobbs House, Federal Express, and International Paper. Memphis also boasts the South's largest medical center, offering highly-specialized health services available in few cities, and the world's largest private hospital, **Baptist Memorial**.

Riverboats along the levee at Memphis.

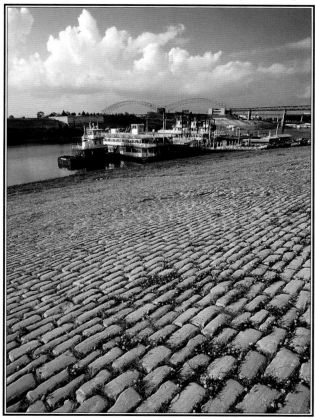

Memphis has a rich history as a cotton trading center. During the mid-19th century, King Cotton bankrolled the city's first wealthy families and their fine mansions. **Cotton Row** on Front St. close to the river docks was the hub of the South's cotton industry, where farmers jammed the street looking for the highest price for their crop. After the Great Depression and World War II, cotton was instrumental in the city's economic recovery. Today Memphis is the largest spot cotton market in the world, with nearly half the United States cotton crop going through the city. Visitors to **Agricenter International**, spread over 1,000 acres in central Memphis, see exhibitions and demonstrations of today's latest agricultural technology.

While famous as the "birthplace of the blues," Memphis is also known as "the biggest town in Mississippi," to north Mississippians. Memphis was designated the northern-most point of the Mississippi

The replica paddlewheeler "Island Queen" departs
for a relaxing pleasure cruise around the city.

On the following pages, the Hernando De Soto Bridge at night.

Delta when author David Cohn wrote, "The Mississippi
Delta begins in the lobby of the Peabody Hotel and
ends on Catfish Row in Vicksburg." A stop by the
posh downtown **Peabody Hotel** is an absolute
tourist-see: every day at precisely 11 a.m. the hotel's
world-renowned mallard ducks parade out of the elevator into the lobby to swim in its fountain. And
every afternoon at five on the dot, they waddle back
across the hotel's red carpet and into the elevator for
the ride to their penthouse pond.
The five-time winner of the Cleanest City in the
Nation title given by the National City Beautiful
Commission, Memphis is a pleasant city to move
around in. The wide streets and a clear street/av-
enue grid system make for easy driving, and a
unique motorcoach transit links attractions, hotels,
parks, and shopping. Major sports events year-
round bring fans to town for the **St. Jude Liberty**

Bowl Football Classic, the Kroger St. Jude International Tennis Championship, the Federal Express St. Jude Golf Classic, the Southern Heritage Classic football game, Team USA Olympic Baseball, the Germantown Charity Horse Show, and others.

Overton Square Entertainment District is a central attraction for visitors for Memphis. In this restored midtown two-block area, you can grab lunch at a gourmet deli, enjoy live music or comedy acts, dance, or browse the many distinctive boutiques. The Cooper Young Entertainment District, a few blocks over, is a diverse arts center of galleries, espresso houses, shops full of unusual clothing, and restaurants featuring international cuisine. A favorite stop in the Cooper Young District is the First Church of The Elvis Impersonator coffee house.

The oldest attraction in town is Chucalissa, a 15th-century Choctaw Indian village administered by the University of Memphis. This carefully-excavated site features an archaeological park, museum, and partially reconstructed village. Choctaw staff members narrate guided tours at Chucalissa and demonstrate crafts.

Hop aboard the electric trolley downtown to visit historic sites and the historic districts of Old Memphis. Historic homes such as the Hunt-Phelan House, built in 1828, reflect the early history of the state as the cotton boom brought prosperity to Mississippi Delta planters. Much of this Beale St. home was built by slave labor; later it was used as part of the Underground Railroad system. The Mallory-Neely House, Woodruff-Fontaine House, and the Magevni House in Victorian Village in downtown Memphis are open to the public, some with

Three views of the Hernando De Soto Bridge.

More bridges across the wide, muddy Mississippi River at Memphis.

changing exhibits featuring period textiles, clothing and fine antiques. The **Pinch Historic District**, also located downtown, was settled in the late 1880s by European immigrants. Take the Main Street Trolley to the Pinch District and visit Old World restaurants, plus quaint antique shops. **A. Schwab's Dry Goods Store** on Beale St. is an 1876 vintage downtown department store, stocking necessities like voodoo potions, a 99-cent necktie, and overalls. Their motto: "If you can't find it at Schwab's, you're better off without it." For more folk culture, stop by the **Center for Southern-Folklore**, also on Beale, and see displays from the Center's large collection of photographs and artifacts. For those interested in cemetery sculpture or monuments to past Memphis luminaries, including "Boss" Crump, a drive through oak-shaded **Elmwood Cemetery** provides a fascinating glimpse of Old Memphis.

The African-American history of Memphis is preserved at numerous sites, among them the **Burkle Estate**, a house built in 1849 by German immigrant Jacob Burkle. Until the end of the Civil War, the house is said to have served as a way station for thousands of runaway slaves on the Underground Railroad. **Auction Square**, in downtown Memphis along Main Street, is the site of the first public market in Memphis; it is speculated that the square's granite marker was used for slave auctioning. Located downtown between the river and Riverside Dr., **Tom Lee Park** is named for a black laborer who in 1925 used a motorboat to rescue 32 people from a sinking river steamer. Lee himself could not swim. **Mason Temple**, where Dr. Martin Luther King, Jr., delivered his famous speech, "I've Been to the Mountain Top," is an important African-American history site. The church, international headquarters for the Church of God in Christ, is also the burial site of the church's founder, Charles H. Mason. The **National Civil Rights Museum** is the first museum to document comprehensively the American civil

The exciting monorail ride to Mud Island.

The famous WWII fighter plane, the Memphis Belle, and the scale model of the river at Mud Island.

Following pages: Mud Island's scale model of the river.

rights movement, from the 1880s to present. The museum was constructed on the site of the **Lorraine Motel** on Mulberry St., below Beale St., where Dr. King was assassinated on April 4, 1968. In addition to artifacts from the civil rights movement, it offers audio-visual displays, interactive exhibits, and an interpretive education center.

Moving from Old Memphis to New Memphis, visitors to the zoo here will not guess that it is, in fact, one of the city's oldest attractions, established in 1906. Many expansions and transformations have taken place since then and today the 70-acre **Memphis Zoo and Aquarium** is home to over 2,800 animals. Cat Country, a free-roaming home for exotic and endangered wild cats, is a popular exhibit, along with the Discovery Center (a hands-on children's museum), an African Veldt, herpetarium, aquarium, tropical birdhouse, and more. Brand new exhibits include the Primate Canyon and Animals of the Night, an exhibit that flips the clock, simulating night for visitors

to watch nocturnal animals' activities during the day. The Memphis Zoo is currently in the midst of yet another renovation that will make it among the world's great zoos.

Flower lovers should schedule a visit to the 96-acre **Memphis Botanic Garden**, featuring the Japanese Garden of Tranquility, the Municipal Rose Garden, the Tennessee Bicentennial Iris Garden, and the Little Garden Club Sensory Garden. Another interesting outdoor area to explore is the **Lichterman Nature Center**, a 65-acre wildlife sanctuary with a three-mile wooded trail, lake and picnic area, greenhouse, and wildlife hospital.

Memphis offers an array of distinguished art museums with changing exhibits and prestigious permanent exhibits. The **Memphis Brooks Museum of Art**, located in Overton Park, is Tennessee's largest museum of ancient and modern-day American and European Art. The Museum offers an important collection of painting, sculpture, prints, drawings, and

78

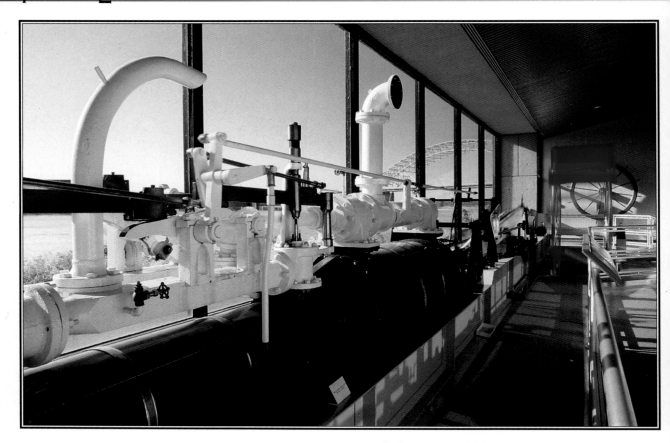

On these pages, exhibits at Mud Island's Mississippi Museum.

photographs, as well as regularly scheduled films and workshops, a museum store, and the Brushmark Restaurant. At the **Dixon Gallery and Gardens**, visitors can view major Impressionist works by Renoir, Degas, and Monet, plus special temporary exhibits on loan from the world's great museums. A walk in the Dixon's beautiful formal garden is an appropriate aesthetic complement to this gallery. Rare Egyptian antiquities and West African art are the specialties of the **Art Museum of the University of Memphis**, which also offers changing exhibits of contemporary art. For natural and cultural history, visit the **Pink Palace Museum and Planetarium** and see its spectacular collection of minerals, dinosaur bones, fossils of 70-million-year-old sea life, and a replicated version of America's first self-serve grocery. (Clarence Saunders, the man who built the Pink Palace, made his fortune in the grocery business.) Covering one of the largest rooms in the museum, the hand-

carved, automated Clyde Parke Miniature Circus keeps visitors busy peering under circus tents to watch the tiny acrobats swing on trapezes and tiny animals jumping hoops. Catch dazzling daily shows at the Pink Palace Planetarium, which puts on an Elvis laser show every August on the anniversary of the death of The King (an occasion widely commemorated in Memphis). Also housed in the Pink Palace is a theater with a movie screen almost five stories high. The Union Planters IMAX movie screen, along with its state-of-the-art motion picture system, projects unusually sharp images onscreen. And seating is close – never more than 50 feet away – so that the IMAX viewing experience is an unforgettable one. A superb sound system matches the visual quality of IMAX, which offers educational adventure films, changing every four or five months. The **Children's Museum of Memphis** is a kid-size discovery museum full of interactive exhibits: children can climb skyscrapers, shop for their own groceries, or drive real cars and motorcycles – all in a child-sized version of a city. Adults are allowed to join in, too, or they can choose to rest while the kids explore. An unusual attraction – or perhaps not, in a city with a particularly famous set of wrought iron gates (Graceland) – is the **National Ornamental Metal Museum**, the only museum in the nation focused on the art of metalworking. A working blacksmith demonstrates the little-known intricacies of metalwork, and exhibits show the result: jewelry, precious metal hollowware, and architectural wrought iron. Take a picnic basket: the grounds of the museum offer a particularly impressive view of the Mississippi River.

Memphis is a city of festivals, hosting over 150 celebrations and special events each year, including a **Zydeco Festival**, **Irish International Street Party**, **Carnival Memphis**, and the **Memphis Blues Festival**. **Africa in April** is a month-long festival

The gleaming new 32-story Pyramid arena celebrates the city's Egyptian namesake.

providing educational programs, music, theater, and art exhibits – all celebrating local African American heritage. The **Memphis in May International Festival** is the largest event of its kind in America. It salutes a different country each year, with programs focused on the culture of that program (Thailand in 1995) and puts on a top-rated music festival on Beale Street. During the May Fest, Memphis, the Pork Barbecue Capital of the World, shows its stuff, with international teams and cooks from the over 100 barbecue restaurants around town competing for the blue ribbon in the **World Championship Barbecue Cooking Contest**.

Memphis is proud of its prestigious **Wonders: the Memphis International Cultural Series**, which has brought fine collections such as "Napoleon," "Rameses the Great," "Splendors of the Ottoman Empire," "The Etruscans," and "Catherine the Great." In 1995 **Wonders** featured "Imperial Tombs of China," an extensive array of spectacular artifacts from the rich tombs of China's great emperors. The 250 objects, from monumental stone guardian lions at the exhibition entrance to a shroud of jade, gold masks and animals, and bronze inlaid figures, made this exhibit a once-in-a-lifetime experience. The **Wonders** Series exhibitions are displayed in the new **Cook Convention Center** in downtown Memphis.

Mid-river by the Memphis bluffs is **Mud Island**, an area that not long ago simply lived up to its name. But now Mud Island is a 52-acre park depicting the history of the Mississippi River, from its source to the Gulf of Mexico. Exhibitions at Mud Island's **Mississippi River Museum** tell the story of the river, beginning 10,000 years ago and carrying visitors past Native American cultures, the Civil War, and up to present-day Memphis and Beale St. A five-block-long miniature Mississippi River, complete with proportionally correct water to wade in, is a refreshing, "feet-on" experience, especially on blistering hot

An electric trolley connects historic districts and sites in Memphis.

An entrance to the Memphis Court House.

summer days. The *Memphis Belle*, World War II's most famous airplane, is restored and displayed under a pavilion on Mud Island. Named for the pilot's wartime sweetheart, the airplane was one of the first to finish 25 missions against Nazi targets without a casualty. The 1943 film *Memphis Belle* – directed by William Wyler – celebrated its story, which is told in exhibits on the site. Mud Island also offers specialty food, shops, and an outdoor amphitheater featuring the best of southern blues, jazz, and rock and roll. Getting to Mud Island is great fun: you glide over on a streamlined monorail that leaves downtown and travels high over the harbor and water, providing a sensational view of the Memphis skyline. (The monorail was central to the chase scene of the movie *The Firm*.)

Across the Mississippi River from Mud Island, the new **Pyramid** juts up from the Memphis skyline, 32 stories of shining stainless steel. This 22,500-seat sports and entertainment arena, its base the size of

six football fields, symbolizes new Memphis – with a bow to the city's Egyptian namesake.

But this is a music town. Practitioners of blues, gospel, rhythm and blues, soul, jazz, and country – they all came to Memphis looking for fame and fortune. Even if they didn't make it financially, these artists (whether they knew it or not at the time) contributed a crucial chapter to the history of American music. It's also a recording town, which is how Memphis really put its name on the music map. From W. C. Handy to Sun Records to Stax and Hi Records, locally-produced recordings of the rich indigenous music of the mid-South have changed the direction of American popular music.

Memphis has nurtured the blues ever since it began being played in the city at the turn of the century. William Christopher Handy, the "Father of the Blues" who lived and worked on Beale St., did not, of course, invent this form of music. Instead, Handy popularized the blues, helping to formalize it by

Rich in music history, Beale St. has been reborn as a vibrant entertainment district.

publishing it, adapting rural blues into his own urban version. In the early 1900s black musicians began to migrate to Memphis, where they played for tips along Beale St. and near the produce market, the present-day site of **Handy Park**. Mostly from the Mississippi Delta, these musicians played harmonica and solo guitar, often bottleneck-style. During the fabled flood of 1937, "rivergee" bluesmen at the Memphis fairgrounds sang the *High Water Blues*:

> *Down at the Fairgrounds on my knees,*
> *Prayin' to the Lord to give me ease –*
> *Lord, Lord, I got them high-water blues!*
>
> *Oh, the river's up and cotton's down,*
> *Mister Ed Crump, he runs this town.*

Another kind of blues was also heard in Memphis: the classic "city blues" brand. These musicians played not in the streets but in prestigious theaters in Memphis and in large halls in other cities. One of

these classic blues singers, born in Memphis in 1895, was Alberta Hunter, who moved to Chicago as a child and there made her first recording in 1921.

Beale St., the "Home of the Blues" and the heart of the city's economy in its early days, almost found itself on the wrong end of a wrecking ball during the 1970s and 1980s, a victim of urban decay. But the street that spurred the creative energy of so many music greats – including Handy, B.B. King, and Elvis Presley – was cherished by Memphians, and the area was saved. Today **Beale Street**, reborn and a National Historic Landmark, offers clubs, cafés, shops, and restored buildings rich in Memphis history. Here W. C. Handy wrote the best of his songs, including *Beale Street Blues* and *Memphis Blues* (which he first wrote as a campaign song for legendary Memphis mayor E. H. "Boss" Crump). The W. C. **Handy Home**, a small shotgun house on Beale St., is now open to the public. The glittering **Orpheum Theatre**, a former vaudeville palace built in 1928, has undergone a $5 million renovation and is today a

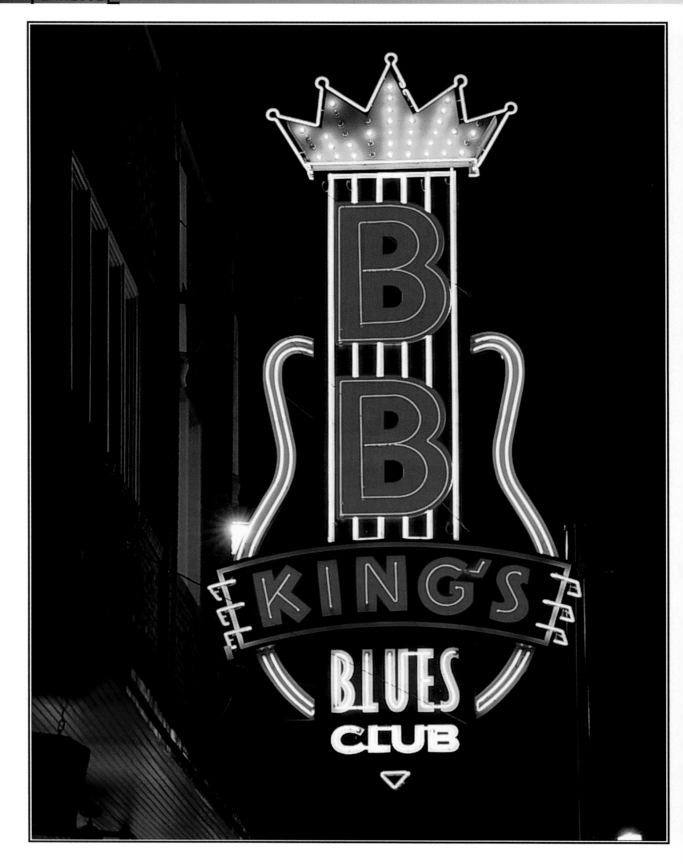

A jam session B.B. King's Blues Club on Beale St.

major center for the performing arts. Nearby are two other restored historic theaters: the famous **Old Daisy**, with its distinctive facade, now houses the **Beale St. Blues Museum**. Across the street at the art deco-style **New Daisy Theatre**, live music (featuring headline blues talent) flows out into the Memphis night. Live music, for that matter, is performed in restaurants and nightspots all along Beale St., such as **B. B. King's Blues Club**, the **Rum Boogie Café, Mr. Handy's Blues Hall**, and the **Blues City Café**. Visitors can listen to outdoor concerts of gospel, blues, jazz, and rock as they tour Handy Park and its Old Memphis brick-street neighborhood in a horse-drawn carriage. In the park, a statue of W. C. Handy, who died in 1958, and a musical walk of fame honor the music and the artists who gave the blues to the world.

Memphis not only nurtured the blues; it was also a major "soul music" center. The birthplace of Aretha Franklin, the city spawned internationally famous soul labels Stax and Hi Records. Stax produced two

sounds: the sixties sound of Rufus and Carla Thomas, Sam and Dave, the Bar-Kays, and Booker T. and the MG's; and the seventies tough-urban sound of Isaac Hayes, which influenced the creation of another musical genre, disco. Hi Records produced a lighter, more sensual sound with artists like Al Green, Ann Peebles, Otis Clay, and O.V. Wright. Sun Records was *the* big Memphis label, a product of the genius of Sam Phillips, who opened his studio in the early 1950s and recorded, first, bluesmen like Howlin' Wolf, Muddy Waters, Big Boy Crudup, B. B. King, and others. His big financial success came later, with country rockers Johnny Cash, Jerry Lee Lewis, Roy Orbison, Carl Perkins and, of course, Elvis Presley. Today tourists stream into the tiny **Sun Studio** to see where it all started. Sun has preserved the original recording equipment and displays photographs, records, and other memorabilia. Be sure to stop by the **Sun Studio Café** next door and have an Elvis special – a fried peanut butter and banana sandwich.

Graceland Mansion in southwest Memphis, beloved home of Elvis Presley, the King of Rock and Roll, opens its wrought-iron gates (decorated with musical notes) to thousands of pilgrims daily. Graceland – a word to conjure with, as Paul Simon and others have demonstrated – has become one of the top tourist attractions in the U.S. since opening in 1982. Fans come to see the rooms Elvis lived in, his refuge for 20 years. Visitors can see Elvis's favorite room, the jungle room, which he decorated in just one day. All the King's memorabilia is gathered in the Trophy Room: his army uniform, favorite Gibson guitar, a collection of his first Sun records, early photographs, and much more. Visitors may think nothing could top the Trophy Room until they step into the Hall of Gold: 37 gold albums, 63 gold singles, and 28 platinum albums representing 100 million record sales. The Meditation Garden, where Elvis and his family are buried, provides a quiet spot for reflection on the man and his world. Those interested in seeing special collections of Elvis's automobiles and private tour jets can continue on the Elvis excursion and reflect later. Another must-see on the Memphis rock and roll tour is the **Jerry Lee Lewis Ranch**, home of the ''Killer,'' in Nesbit, Mississippi, a short drive from downtown Memphis. Lewis has displayed here for visitors a large selection of personal memorabilia including photographs and gold records. Lewis' piano-shaped pool alone is worth the drive.

Left, above: The King of Rock and Roll in his heyday.

Left: Graceland.

Right, above: The Hall of Gold at Graceland: 37 gold albums, 63 gold singles, and 28 platinum albums.

Below: Elvis memorabilia on display at Graceland, and the King's grave.

Previous pages: Once hand-picked by slaves, vast acres of Delta cotton are now harvested mechanically every fall.

Clarksdale's Delta Blues Museum features a life-sized wax figure.

CLARKSDALE

A right turn off Beale St. in downtown Memphis takes you straight down to Clarksdale on Highway 61, as the Great River Road is called in these parts. This is the legendary blues highway, snaking along the river through the state of Mississippi's Delta.

The Delta, as it's simply called here, is a land apart – a distinct region within the entire Mississippi River delta. For eons the river has flooded every spring, its waters leaving behind deposits of silt and sediment. Today the river's delta – covering two million acres along both sides of the river from Illinois to the Gulf of Mexico – is some of the world's richest agricultural land. Mississippi's Delta is a flat rural expanse of great impoverishment amid great cotton plantations, an incongruous place – both harsh and romantic.

This is the same contradiction of the blues, which emerged here 100 years ago. Memphis may lay claim as the "birthplace of the blues," but this deeply-felt, restless, resigned, down-and-out sound first came into being under a blazing sun in Delta fields, sung by black farmworkers "choppin'" and picking cotton.

W.C. Handy carried the blues to Memphis and the world from his Clarksdale home. He is one of a remarkable number of musicians from Mississippi, including Robert Johnson, Son House, Charlie Patton, Muddy Waters, Howlin' Wolf, and John Lee Hooker. Clarksdale's **Delta Blues Museum** celebrates this heritage with exhibits, videos, performances, and archives. One exhibit, "All Shook Up: Mississippi Roots of American Popular Music," explores Mississippi's extraordinary contribution to blues, country music, gospel, R&B, rock and roll, and jazz. Get the actual recordings (and more blues lore) at Stackhouse/Delta Record Mart. At blues clubs – "juke joints" – in Clarksdale and around the Delta, the real thing is performed live. Or tune to radio station **WROX**: Early "The Soul Man" Wright has been broadcasting the blues here since 1947.

PORT GIBSON

Unlike many southern hamlets in the path of northern armies during the Civil War, Port Gibson was spared, supposedly called "too beautiful to burn" by Union Gen. Ulysses S. Grant. Today the town celebrates its historic good fortune annually during **Spring Pilgrimage**, which opens private antebellum homes to the public.

Throughout the year a visit to Port Gibson is a foray back to the 19th-century smalltown South. Downtown walking tours are recommended (if the weather is not sultry), with descriptive markers on significant homes and buildings informing the way. You'll find tour headquarters on Church St. at the town's oldest existing structure, the **Samuel Gibson House** (ca. 1805), now the Chamber of Commerce. Down the street is **Oak Square**, a 30-room mansion built in 1850. There are also eight 19th-century churches of interest on Church St., including the unusual Moorish/Byzantine-style **Temple Gemiluth Chessed** and **First Presbyterian Church**, with its famous steeple topped by a 10-foot golden hand pointing to heaven.

Port Gibson's history is captured in an exhibit, "Picturing Our Past: Photographs from the Allen Collection 1906-1915," on display at the **Port Gibson City Hall**. Included are more than 50 images of everyday life recorded by a local photographer in the early 20th-century.

In a lonely clearing near the river, a few miles outside Port Gibson, are the haunting ruins of **Windsor**, built in 1861. All that remains of this once-magnificent five-story Greek Revival mansion are 23 towering Corinthian columns. Windsor survived the Civil War; a cigarette tossed by a careless house guest is said to have caused its destruction by fire in 1890. Down the road is the ghost town of **Rodney**, a prosperous cotton port until the Mississippi changed course. Nearby is **Grand Gulf**, another once-busy – and now landlocked – port destroyed by yellow fever, storms, Yankee gunboats, and the meanderings of the river. Today it's the site of **Grand Gulf Military Monument Park**, which includes a Civil War museum, battlegrounds, observation tower, and hiking trails. Stop at **Lorman** (between Port Gibson and Natchez) for an authentic slice of Americana at **The Old Country Store**, in business since 1890. Also near Lorman is **Rosswood Plantation**, an 1857 Greek Revival plantation home, now a bed and breakfast. Designed by the architect of Windsor, Rosswood has 14-foot ceilings, 10 fireplaces, and 14 rooms furnished with fine antiques.

The haunting ruins of Windsor.

A golden hand points heaven-ward atop Port Gibson's First Presbyterian Church.

The Battle of Vicksburg was a turning point in the Civil War.

VICKSBURG

After a brutal 47-day siege, Confederate Vicksburg fell to Union forces on July 4, 1863. This won the North control of the Mississippi River and turned the tide in its war to subdue rebellious southern states. Until fairly recently, the 4th of July was not celebrated in Vicksburg.

Lofty 200-foot river bluffs determined the strategic importance of the town, called the "Gibraltar of the Confederacy." Today, the Campaign for Vicksburg is vividly recalled at the lush, rolling 1,800-acre **Vicksburg National Military Park**. Here cannons still stand ready to fire on ironclad Yankee gunboats upon the river. Rebel fortifications have been maintained, and the bloody Union advance is traced with informative markers. Throughout the park are beautiful monuments and impressive statues erected by states who sent soldiers to Vicksburg. The elegiac, domed **Illinois Monument**, built in 1906, is inscribed with the names of the thousands of Illinois soldiers who fought here. The **USS Cairo**, a Union ironclad

gunboat sunk by Confederates, is on display in the park, raised and restored after 100 years under water. An adjacent museum displays artifacts recovered from the *Cairo*, including clothing, dishes, and – remarkably – a watch that still runs. Approximately 17,000 Union soldiers are buried at the **Vicksburg National Cemetery**, part of the national park. The **Vicksburg City Cemetery** is the final resting place for many Confederate dead.

A number of the city's antebellum structures are open to the public. The **Duff Green Mansion**, built in 1856 and now an elegant bed and breakfast, served as a Civil War hospital. (During the siege of Vicksburg, Mrs. Green gave birth to a son, named Siege.) The Greek Revival **Old Court House Museum**, built by slaves in 1858, housed Union prisoners during the siege and thus avoided severe shelling. Today it is a historical museum, with emphasis on the city's Civil War era. Begun in the late 1700's, **McRaven** was built in three periods: Frontier,

The Illinois Monument in the Vicksburg National Military Park.

Vicksburg's Old Court House housed Union prisoners during the siege of the city during the Civil War.

Following pages: An inviting veranda at Rosswood Plantation.

Empire, and Greek Revival. Highlights of any tour of McRaven are its museum-quality antiques and its cannon damage – inside and out. **Balfour House**, built in 1835, was the home of Emma Balfour, a famous civil war diarist.

After the fall of Vicksburg, Balfour House became Union Headquarters; today it's a bed and breakfast. **Cedar Grove** (ca. 1840) is an opulent 30-room inn situated on four garden acres overlooking the Mississippi River.

Civil War re-enactments and period dances are regularly staged by local historical societies. "The Vanishing Glory," a 30-minute wide-screen audio-visual dramatization of the Campaign for Vicksburg, is shown on the hour at the Waterfront Theatre. River buffs will want to visit the **Waterways Experiment Station** the primary research facility for the U.S. Army Corps of Engineers. See here working scale models of major U.S. waterways, such as Niagara Falls and the Mississippi.

Longwood is the largest octagonal house in the U.S.

"King" Cotton is still Mississippi's most important agricultural product.

Three historical images illustrating the importance of the Mississippi river for cotton transportation.

LONGWOOD

There's something both lovely and sad about **Longwood**, the unfinished Oriental-style mansion found on the outskirts of Natchez. The Civil War halted the slow, meticulous construction of Longwood, the largest octagonal house in the U.S., and destroyed the fortune and health of its builder, Dr. Haller Nutt (an ardent Union sympathizer). Today the completed basement floor is furnished with family heirlooms. The ornate upper five levels remain a shell, and construction tools can be seen where they fell over hundred years ago when the war forced northern workers home.

The builder of Natchez's Stanton Hall chartered an entire ship to import European furnishings and materials.

Elaborate ornamental iron grillwork at Stanton Hall.

NATCHEZ

The Mississippi River brought great riches to Natchez, once the largest river port above New Orleans. In its heyday, which lasted from the docking of the first Mississippi River steamboat (the *New Orleans*) here in 1811 to the outbreak of the Civil War in 1860, Natchez boasted over 500 millionaires, more than any other town in the U.S. except New York City. This affluent aristocracy used slave labor to build opulent townhouses, churches, public buildings, and grand plantation homes – and all escaped destruction in the Civil War. More than 500 local antebellum structures survive to this day – many beautifully restored and standing as elegant testimony to the "Golden Age of Natchez."

Established by the French in 1716 as Fort Rosalie, Natchez is the oldest permanent settlement on the Mississippi. It is the terminus for the legendary **Natchez Trace**, the centuries-old wilderness road stretching 500 miles northwest to Nashville. First traveled by Indians, then European explorers and settlers, the Natchez Trace served as the overland return route of "kaintucks." Before the invention of the steamboat, these northern and mid-western flat-

boatmen rafted their wares down the Mississippi River, then walked home. Today the scenic Natchez Trace Parkway is carefully maintained by the National Park Service, and runs 313 miles diagonally across the state of Mississippi.

The city of Natchez got its name from the Natchez Indians, sun-worshipers who lived here before the arrival of whites in some 30-odd villages along the Mississippi River bluffs. Their chief settlement, called Grand Village by the French, was built along Saint Catherine's Creek and is now an archaeological park and museum. The **Grand Village of The Natchez Indians**, which features several earth mounds and a reconstructed Natchez house, is located within the Natchez city limits, open daily. West of the Natchez Trace near Natchez is **Emerald Mound**, the 2nd-largest ceremonial Indian mound in the country. Built around 1300 A.D. by ancestors of the Natchez and Choctaw Indians, the eight-acre site is 35 feet-high at its flat summit, offering a commanding view of the surrounding countryside.

Early Natchez grew up around the river landing below Natchez Bluff known as **Natchez-Under-the**

A bridge across the Mississippi River at Natchez.

Hill. By the early 1800s the area was a notorious center of gambling and vice, reputedly the "Barbary Coast of the Mississippi" or the "Cesspool of the South." Most of this once-rowdy haunt of murderous outlaws, card sharks, and ladies of the evening has been eroded away by the river. The rustic historic district that remains down by the river today, primarily along Silver St., is the site of shops, bars, restaurants, and – appropriately – riverboat casino gambling.

Natchez's black history is celebrated at the **Natchez Museum of African-American History and Culture**, which houses a 600-piece permanent exhibit of African-American historical artifacts dating from 1890 through the 1950s. The **Mostly African Market** sells African and African-American arts and crafts. Information on a self-guided tour of African-American points of interest is available from the Natchez Convention and Visitors Bureau.

But beautiful old homes are the main event here. Come for the annual spring or fall **Natchez Pilgrimage**, when private antebellum mansions are open to the public, hosted by hoop-skirted ladies and men in period costumes. The Pilgrimages are important social events in Natchez, complete with grand balls and pageants, but come anytime of the year: numerous architectural treasures are year-round tourist attractions, many offering charming bed and breakfast accommodations. Because there is so much to see here (over 1,000 Natchez structures are on the National Register of Historic Places) guided tours are a good idea. Fifty-minute double-decker bus tours cost $10 and depart Monday through Saturday on the hour from downtown at Canal and State streets. Horse-drawn carriage tours of historic downtown begin daily at the Natchez Pilgrimage Tour Headquarters on Canal St., or evenings at the elegant **Natchez Eola Hotel**. The city transit system operates a motorized downtown trolley costing 50 ¢ a ride; $1 daily passes are also available.

The climate in Natchez is generally mild (although it does get hot in summer), and a walking tour through the **Natchez Downtown Historic District** is usually a pleasant option. (A map of downtown can be found in the *Tourists' Guide to Historic Natchez*, available at hotels, restaurants, and information centers.) You'll stroll past sixteen blocks of antique shops, restaurants, lovely old homes, historic churches – and some of the South's most palatial antebellum mansions. Occupying an entire city block shaded by ancient oaks is magnificent **Stanton Hall**, built in 1858 and renowned for its elaborate iron grillwork and 72-foot central hallway. Its builder, an Irishman named Frederick Stanton, chartered an entire ship to import the finest European furnishings and building materials to his Natchez home. **Rosalie**, dating from 1820, is a splendid brick Georgian house, open daily to the public. Set high upon a river palisade, Rosalie is near the site of the original Fort Rosalie and served as Union army headquarters during the Civil War. Across the street is **The Parsonage**, built by the master of Rosalie to house his enthusiastically religious wife's itinerate friends in the ministry. **Texada**, built in 1792, is today an inn in the **Old Spanish Quarter**, and was the first brick house in the Mississippi territory. **The House on Ellicott's Hill** (also known as Connelly's Tavern) has seen its share of famous guests, including the traitorous Aaron Burr. The American flag was first raised here in defiance of Spain in 1797. **The Wigwam**, which dates from between 1790-1856, is now a romantic bed and breakfast. (Some consider The Wigwam the loveliest antebellum mansion in town.) A fine example of early, pure Greek Revival design, **The Burn**, dated 1836, is noted for the beautiful semi-spiral staircase in its central hall and its rare camellia gardens. The last great mansion constructed here before the Civil War, **Magnolia Hall** (built in 1858) is one of the few Natchez structures to have been damaged by shells fired from a Union gunboat.

Near downtown is **Dunleith**, an 1856 Greek Revival mansion set on 40 landscaped acres dotted with stables and plantation outbuildings. Reminiscent of a Greek temple, Dunleith is surrounded on four sides by galleries and 26 huge columns. Red-bricked **Auburn** was built in 1812. Located in **Duncan City Park**, the old home is famous for its exquisite free-standing spiral staircase and other architecturally significant details. Its builder, New Yorker Levi Weeks, observed that Auburn was the "first house in the Mississippi Territory on which was attempted any of the orders of Architecture." *U.S.A Today* and *Glamour* magazine rate **Monmouth Plantation**, erected in 1818, as among the "Top 10 Most Romantic Places in the U.S." Built on 26 flawlessly-manicured garden acres, Monmouth is an imposing brick mansion originally home to Gen. John A. Quitman, an early state governor, war hero, and congressman.

On this and on following pages: A riverboat casino docked at Natchez-Under-the-Hill.

Baton Rouge, the Governor's House, in the typical style of the ''Antebellum mansion''.

BATON ROUGE

How the city of Baton Rouge got its name is unclear. One legend has it that local Indians hung their game on a tall slim tree, which became stained with blood. French visitors to the Indians' village supposedly saw this and named the settlement *Le Baton Rouge* or ''The Red Stick.'' Another legend cites a large cypress growing out of the bluff above the river. This particular tree's bark is said to have been removed, giving it a red color – *Le Baton Rouge* – that served as a vivid boundary marker between Houma and Bayou Goula tribal territories.

Baton Rouge is approximately 80 miles northwest of New Orleans, set strategically upon a bluff above the Mississippi River. In 1718, the French set out to build a fort here to protect travelers en route to and from New Orleans. Through the centuries, seven flags have flown over Baton Rouge, officially chartered as a city in 1817. Today it is the capital of Louisiana.

Early in this century, Baton Rouge began to develop industrially; the city is now the center of the South's petrochemical industry. Here the Exxon Corporation manufactures more than 700 products from petroleum and operates one of the world's largest oil refineries. Baton Rouge is the farthest inland deep-water port of the Gulf of Mexico – some 230 water miles from the mouth of the Mississippi River. The city is also home to Louisiana State University and Southern University, the largest predominantly black university in the U.S. At **LSU** see the **Rural Life Museum**, featuring a working plantation. Located near LSU and the river is an authentically restored French Creole house, **Magnolia Mound Plantation**, built in the early 1790s.

The biggest attraction in town is the 34-story Art

Deco **Louisiana State Capitol**. Built in 1932 by the colorful controversial Governor Huey P. Long, this is also where he was assassinated in 1935. Long is buried in the capitol gardens. Inside the capitol is a treasure trove of bronze and marble decoration depicting Louisiana's history. The building's 27th floor observation deck provides a grand view of Baton Rouge and the Mississippi.

The Gothic Revival **Old State Capitol**, built in 1849, recently underwent a $16 million renovation and is now Louisiana's Center for Political and Governmental History. Also known as "Louisiana Castle," its architectural highlights include an iron circular staircase and stained-glass rotunda. The 40-room **Governor's Mansion** was built in 1963 to resemble an antebellum plantation house. The real thing can be seen at **Nottoway**, 16 miles south of Baton Rouge. This Greek Revival and Italianate mansion (built in 1859) is the largest surviving plantation home in the South, with 64 rooms, 200 windows, and 165 doors. Twenty-two columns support the front verandas. Nottoway is now a restaurant; daily tours are available, as well as overnight accommodations.

A detail of the colonnade of the Governor's House.

*San Francisco Plantation was built in the exuberant
Steamboat Gothic style.*

LOUISIANA PLANTATION COUNTRY

Below Natchez, the **River Road** winds east and west of the Mississippi River through Baton Rouge to New Orleans.

Along the way are sumptuous restored antebellum homes, survivors of a time when many grand cotton and sugar plantations were maintained upriver from New Orleans by prosperous planters. A leisurely drive through **Plantation Country**, as this stretch of the River Road is called, is an ideal way to see these lovely old places, shaded by ancient gnarled live oaks draped in Spanish moss. A number of sites are open to the public and several have become bed and breakfasts or restaurants. But while savoring the ambience of a bygone era, be prepared for some jolts back into the 20th century: along this stretch of the River Road, flat fields where cotton and sugar cane once grew are now dotted with flame-topped oil facilities.

About 25 miles south of Baton Rouge on the east side of the Mississippi is St. Francisville, where most of

the town seems to be on the National Register of Historic Places.

Make an early stop at the **West Feliciana Historical Museum**, which provides sightseers with a helpful map of local points of interest. Wildlife painter John James Audubon spent time here in the 1820s, and some of his work is displayed at the **Audubon Art Gallery** at the Best Western-St. Francisville Hotel. South of town is the **Audubon State Commemorative Area**, which includes **Oakley House**, where Audubon served as a tutor and painted much of his *Birds of America* series. Opulent **Rosedown Plantation and Historic Garden**, a bed and breakfast set on 28 acres of celebrated gardens, is a *de rigueur* tourist stop. Built between 1835 and 1858, Rosedown features a Gothic bedroom suite originally intended for Henry Clay, upon his election to the U.S. presidency. Clay, however, lost the election of 1844 and his erstwhile gift was sent to Rosedown, whose owner

The lovely quarter-mile canopy of live oaks fronting Oak Alley Plantation.

added a new wing to the house to accommodate this enormous furniture.

Across the Mississippi and farther down River Road is romantic **Oak Alley Plantation**, built around 1839. The main house is an impressive columned Creole-Greek structure, but Oak Alley is most famous for its facing rows of arching live oak trees, 14 on each side. Planted in the early 1700s by a French settler, this *allée* creates a breathtaking quarter-mile canopy stretching from the front of the house to the river. Oak Alley has been the setting of several Hollywood movies, including *The Long Hot Summer* and *Interview With the Vampire*. Exuberant **San Francisco**, built in 1854, is on the east side of the river closer to New Orleans. Extravagantly decorated at great expense, this outlandish house was designed to look like a steamboat, hence its architectural style: "Steamboat Gothic." Inside, note the artistically marbleized and grained cypress millwork and huge ceiling frescoes of painted wood.

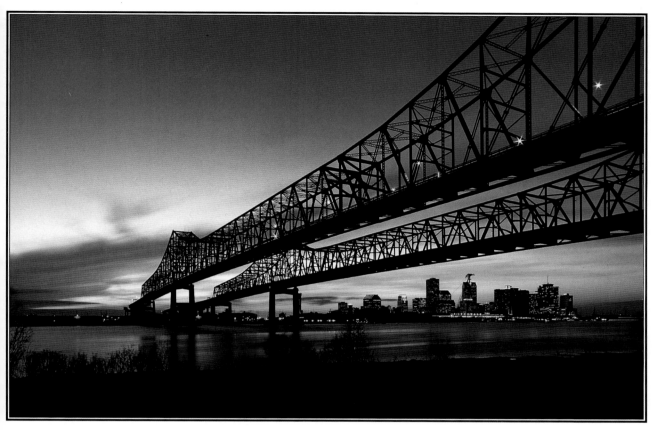

An aerial view of the New Orleans riverfront alongside the Moon Walk and Jackson Square.

The twin spans of the Mississippi River bridge.

NEW ORLEANS

New Orleans, the most exotic place on the Mississippi River, is also the most exotic American city. For more than four centuries, the Mississippi has poured people of widely different races and nationalities into the "Crescent City" (so-called because of its location in a sharp bend in the river). The 1860 Census tells the tale: according to official records at that time 41 percent of New Orleans residents were foreign-born, representing 32 nations – not to mention the influx from distinctly disparate sections of the United States. The mix, in part, included Indians, Spanish, French ("Creoles"), Africans, Germans, Irish, flatboatmen from the upper Mississippi River Valley ("kaintucks"), Italians, Latin Americans, English, Portuguese, Greeks, Orientals, and New Yorkers (who, some theorize, brought "wit dem" the Brooklyn-esque accent oddly prevalent in New Orleans today).

Along with this motley human contribution to the character of New Orleans, founded in 1718 by Jean-Baptiste le Moyne, Sieur de Bienville, the Mississippi River has brought the city commerce and wealth. It was, in fact, New Orleans' importance as a river port that led to that monumental real estate deal, the Louisiana Purchase. (President Thomas Jefferson could hardly countenance French or Spanish control over a port so vital to American trade.) The American flag was first raised over the immense territory obtained by the U.S. in the Louisiana Purchase in the **Place d'Armes**, now known as **Jackson Square**. This public square faces the Mississippi River and forms the base of the **French Quarter**, or **Vieux Carré**, laid out by Bienville in 1721. Imposing **St. Louis Cathedral** stands on Jackson Square opposite the river; its central spire is the tallest structure in the Quarter. The cathedral is flanked by two historic Spanish colonial buildings, the **Cabildo** and the **Presbytère**. The graceful twin **Pontabla Buildings**, believed to be the first apartment buildings in the U.S., face one

115

Riverboats on the Mississippi at New Orleans.

another on the other sides of the square. In the center is the ten-ton equestrian statue of **Gen. Andrew Jackson**, hero of the Battle of New Orleans in the War of 1812, for whom this plaza is named.

The first commercial steamboat on the Mississippi, the *New Orleans*, docked here on January 10, 1812. Between this date and the beginning of the Civil War, New Orleans became the world's greatest export center, primarily shipping cotton and sugar produced upriver by vast plantations sustained by slave labor. Great fortunes were made during this boom, and many newly-rich merchants and businessmen built grand antebellum mansions in the beautiful **Garden District** close to downtown. These magnificent homes stand today, most in their original condition, most still occupied by some of the city's wealthiest citizens. Garden District residences are typically private, but architectural sight-seeing in the neighborhood is easy – just hop aboard the St. Charles Ave. streetcar.

St. Louis Cathedral facing Jackson Square.

The 10-ton equestrian statue of Andrew Jackson in Jackson Square.

A montage of jazz images in New Orleans.

Much of New Orleans is several feet below sea level and would be below water altogether if not for the system of levees Mark Twain once described as a "frail breastwork of earth between the people and destruction." And during flood season, rain water is as much of a hazard as river water. When heavy weather hits – as it does frequently in this sub-tropical, hurricane-prone climate – pumps must be used to drain over-accumulations of rain water out of the city. The fact that New Orleans is below sea level also explains its unusual, eerie above-ground cemeteries, or **Cities of The Dead**.

A perfect place to view the Mississippi River is directly below Jackson Square at the **Moon Walk**, named for former mayor Moon Landrieu. Here see jaunty tugboats and foreign freighters cruise by, carrying cargo to and from the **Port of New Orleans**. More than 2,500 ships from all over the globe call here every year, and most authorities rank New Orleans the nation's 2nd largest port, after New York

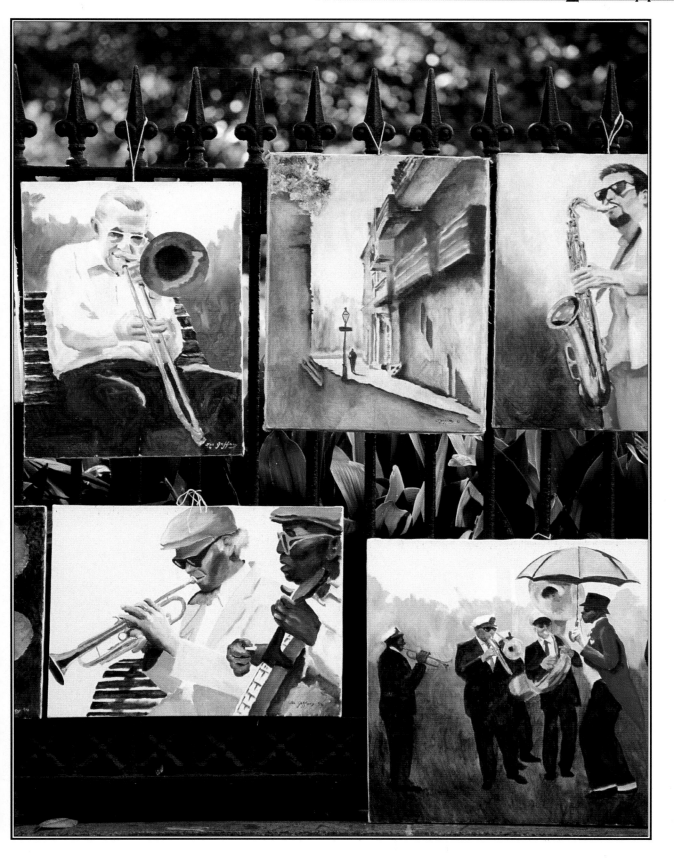

*Fancy iron grillwork is a classic architectural feature of the
French Quarter.*

City. With 12 miles of riverside wharves, this is the
3rd most commercially productive port in the world.
A variety of riverboats dock at the Moon Walk, including the *Creole Queen* and *Cajun Queen*, which
cruise six miles down to Chalmette, Louisiana, to the
site of the Battle of New Orleans. Children especially
enjoy the *John James Audubon*, which makes stops at
New Orleans' outstanding wildlife attractions, the
Audubon Zoo and the **Aquarium of the Americas**.
After dark, the steam sternwheeler *Natchez* offers a
jazz dinner cruise.
Yet for all the economic bustle and varied humanity
brought in by the mighty Mississippi, the city of New
Orleans often seems more like some languid river
oxbow in summertime: the "land of dreamy
dreams," to use singer Louis Armstrong's apt
phrase. In the same vein, another nickname for New
Orleans is "The Big Easy." The pace is relaxed, the
atmosphere casual – a pleasing vestige of the city's
European heritage. (Certainly hot, humid weather a

good part of the year does its part to slow things
down.) This laid-back romanticism has long attracted
artists and writers, from William Faulkner to
Tennessee Williams, who lived in the French
Quarter. Today the city lends uncanny inspiration to
Anne Rice, best-selling author of *Interview with the
Vampire*. Literary afficianados will enjoy guided
tours of the homes and hang-outs of famous writers.
Fans of Rice, note the tour of local haunted houses.
Not that anybody in New Orleans is too relaxed to
have a good time. And, certainly, the good times *really* roll every year during **Mardi Gras**, the city's
epic annual pre-Lenten carnival. But all through the
year, the world-renowned bars on raucous **Bourbon
St.** virtually never close. Without a doubt, the city is
sensational feast for all types of music-lovers. Jazz
was born here, an unfettered blend of African
rhythms and European horns. Whether from clubs
showcasing world-famous artists or the blare of a
curb-side trumpeter, the sounds of jazz provide a

Nightclubs fill New Orleans with the sounds of jazz, rock, and rhythm and blues.

constant soundtrack for the French Quarter. At **Preservation Hall** on St. Peter St., you can still hear jubilant traditional Dixieland jazz. Hit **Pete Fountain's** at the New Orleans Hilton Riverside and spend some time with the master of the jazz clarinet. New Orleans legend Ernie "Mother-in-Law" K Doe appears every Sunday night at his club, the **First Stop Lounge**. **Tipitina's** on Napoleon St. is the place to catch the hometown Neville Brothers, and other top R&B and rock performers. Every April and May, the **New Orleans Jazz and Heritage Festival** attracts hundreds of thousands of exuberant music lovers from all over the world.

Eating is also a joyous pastime in The Big Easy, named "Best Food City in the World" in the Conde Nast 1994 Traveler's Poll. As with music, the city's wide-ranging multi-culturalism has had an altogether salutary effect on the indigenous cuisine, which ultimately blended into unique styles of creole and cajun cooking. Happily, this distinctive, spicy fare is a

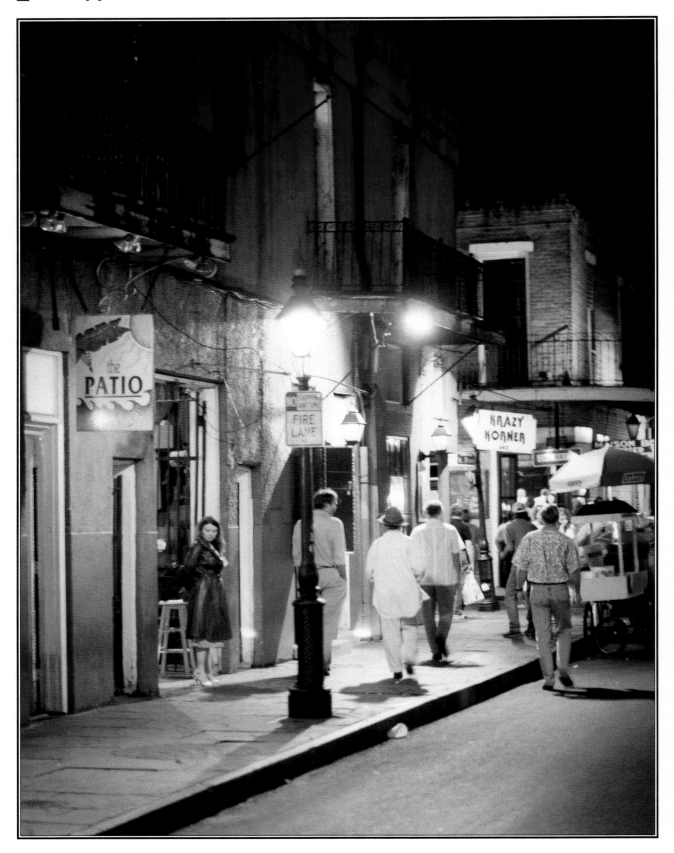

The bars on raucous Bourbon St. virtually never close.

gastronomic delight just about anywhere you choose to pick up a fork in New Orleans – from the fanciest dining room to the lowliest dive. **Galatoire's** on Bourbon St., operated by the same family since 1905, is one of the finest restaurants in the country. You know it's first-rate, because you'll be standing in line to get in (no reservations accepted – no exceptions, ever) with as many locals as tourists. **Chez Helène**, located well off the beaten path, serves down-home soul food and creole dishes as unpretentious as they are sublime. Steaming café au lait and hot beignets dusted with powdered sugar are served 24 hours a day at **Café du Monde** on Decatur St. along the riverfront. Even brown-bagging is a gustatory pleasure in New Orleans. Prove it to yourself by picking up a fried oyster po-boy sandwich and a bottle of Dixie Beer at any neighborhood eatery.

The Mississippi River separates into three channels as it nears the Gulf of Mexico, creating a "birdfoot" delta.

DOWN TO THE GULF

South of New Orleans, the Mississippi River current slows, and its width narrows from more than a mile across to less than 1,000 feet. As it nears the end of its steam at the **Head of Passes**, the river separates into three channels (**Southwest Pass**, **South Pass**, and **Pass a Loutre**) creating a geographic configuration known as the "birdfoot." Now the prodigious load of sediment borne over 2,500 miles, infused by myriad feeder streams and great muddy rivers like the Missouri and the Ohio, becomes too heavy to be carried by the current and sinks to the bottom. Over thousands of years this process created southern Louisiana; in the last several centuries it added many square miles of boggy lowlands to the southeastern tip of the state.

These continuous deposits have in times past threatened to close the passes entirely, blocking the river to the Gulf of Mexico and international shipping. In the mid-1800s conventional dredging efforts began

to lose this battle entirely. Dangerous wrecks narrowed the way, and ships going to and from the Gulf had to be towed at high tide over sandbars and mud. The public demanded the federal government to take action. 1875, at the direction of the U.S. Congress, Capt. James B. Eades – the self-educated engineering genius who built the celebrated Eades Bridge at St. Louis – set to work on a system of parallel jetties that would force the river to scour a deeper channel at its mouth. His ambitious project was plagued by financial difficulties, while yellow fever took its deadly toll on his men. But after four years, a 30-foot deep, quarter-mile-wide channel at South Pass opened the river into the Gulf of Mexico. Today all large vessels come through here or the 40-foot deep Southwest Pass.

The Mississippi's birdfoot delta is a huge brackish swamp rich with plant and animal life – and five species of poisonous snakes. It is the last stop on the

Where tide waters meet the Mississippi River current, a vast estuary is formed.

Mississippi Flyway for the hundreds of thousands of migratory birds that winter here, along with indigenous waterfowl like the brown sea pelican. For years the region's most exotic resident, the alligator, was over-hunted and near extinction; now the reptile's population has resurged, thanks to strict federal poaching prohibitions. Another unusual species, the South American nutria, has been extensively trapped for its fur pelt, yet still reproduces at a rate alarming (and infuriating) to many locals.

Where tide waters meet the culminating Mississippi currents, a vast estuary is formed. Fishing, shrimping, and oyster beds are major industries, while tourists come to fish and experience this isolated, distinctive region up close. The towns of Venice (the southern-most point on the Great River Road) and Grand Isle offer beaches, camping, motels, and boat charters. Much of the area is maintained as wildlife preserves, including the **Breton National Wildlife Refuge**, **Delta National Wildlife Refuge**, and the

Pass a Loutre Wildlife Management Area – 66,000 acres of wetland accessible only by boat.

In an often uneasy coexistence, nature and the oil industry go about their business here side-by-side. From Baton Rouge south, oil companies operate huge oil fields and flaming refineries. Thousands of off-shore oil rigs dot the Gulf of Mexico. And here, flood and erosion control is a constant, high-stakes battle. The Mississippi River wants to move west and flow down the shorter Achafalaya River basin to the Gulf of Mexico. Engineering efforts have been underway for decades to stave off this potentially devastating deviation. Whether or not one believes man will prevail in this battle is a matter of faith in modern technology. But there are those who would bet on the river: "One might as well bully the comets in their courses," wrote Mark Twain in *Life on the Mississippi*, "and undertake to make them behave, as try to bully the Mississippi into right and reasonable conduct."

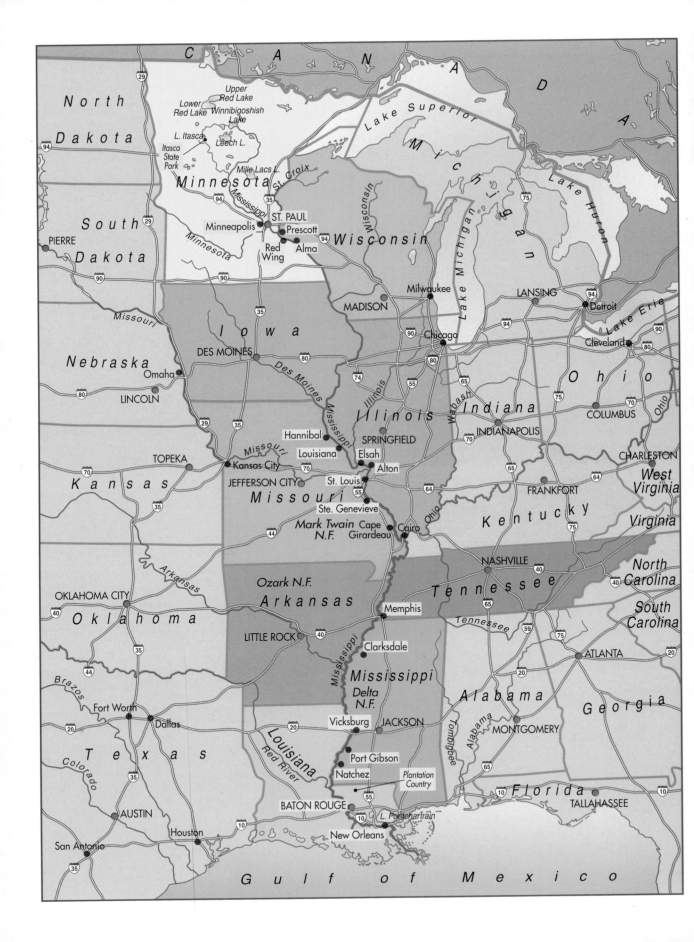